UNCONVENTIONAL WISDOM

UNCONVENTIONAL
WISDOM

TWELVE
REMARKABLE
INNOVATORS
TELL HOW
INTUITION
CAN
REVOLUTIONIZE
DECISION
MAKING

RON
SCHULTZ

HarperBusiness
A Division of HarperCollins*Publishers*

HarperCollins books may be purchased for educational, business, or sales promotional use. For information please write: Special Markets Department, HarperCollins Publishers, Inc., 10 East 53rd Street, New York, NY 10022.

FIRST EDITION

Designed by Alma Hochhauser Orenstein

Library of Congress Cataloging-in-Publication Data

Schultz, Ron (Ronald), 1951–
    Unconventional wisdom: twelve remarkable innovators tell how intuition can revolutionize decision making/by Ron Schultz.
        p. cm.
    Includes index.
    ISBN 0-88730-651-9
    1. Management—Case studies. 2. Intuition (Psychology)—Case studies. I. Title.
    HD38.S3674 1994
    658.4'03—dc20   93-36431

94 95 96 97 98 ❖/HC 10 9 8 7 6 5 4 3 2 1

This book is dedicated to:
Johana, Emily, Laura, Christie, and Peggy

CONTENTS

ACKNOWLEDGMENTS

EXPERIENCE AND KNOWLEDGE are the cornerstone for successful intuitive responses. Fortunately for me, I had some remarkable people to speak with who were able to impart their knowledge and experience to me. Without their time, efforts, and ability to articulate what they know this book could never have been written. It is with great appreciation that I thank them now.

From the world of business, these decision makers opened their thoughts, perceptions, and actions to me: Regis McKenna, Don Richard, Richard Schwartz, Michael Brown, Bijan Amini, Barbara Hendra, Ted Doster, Al Silverman, Robert Tirone, Victor Kiam, Herbert Conrad, Pete Dawkins, Helen Gurley Brown, Michael Silva, and Lillian Vernon.

From the psychological community, I had the opportunity to speak with two very profound, intuitive, and caring men, whose input was of immense value to this project: Dr. Joseph B. Wheelwright and Dr. Robert Johnson.

In the entertainment and sports worlds I was provided with a source that spoke directly to the intuitive function. Stephen J. Cannell, Phyllis Tucker Vinson, Perry Lafferty, Gordon Davidson, Robert Fraley, Joe Gibbs, Gene Bartow, Al Campanis, and Jack McKeon, all offered me their candid stories and perceptions.

The scientific and medical communities have long valued the intuitive leap that can carry a scientist into vast, uncharted areas of discovery. I am very grateful to Lew Allen, Bruce Murray, Murray Gell-Mann, Edmund Rutsky, Frank Hughes, Phillip R. Fine, and Seymour Papert for their willingness to speak beyond the mere logic of things and address what Murray Gell-Mann has referred to as, "The soaring of the human spirit."

Politics demands a quick mind, able to assimilate and synthesize a variety of different and disparate ideas. A politician must then be able to articulate a position based on those issues at almost any given moment. These excellent minds provided an invaluable service to this book in this area: Edmund G. "Jerry" Brown Jr., Senator John Chaffee, E. Allison Thomas, Charles Grattick, Fredrick Downs, and Dee Fine.

In addition to those whose interviews supplied a great deal of the knowledge base for this book, there were others who contributed a different kind of support. The development of this project is due in no small part to the combined efforts of Lisa Cron, Ken Luboff, Ken Clements, Barbara Hendra, Karen Farrell, Julie Marshall, Judy Hubner, and Norm Levine, with a special thanks to Sam Schultz. Their vision, comments, and support helped launch this project, and kept me afloat during the long voyage.

Then there are the administrative assistants and communication directors who were of particular help to me in setting up time with those whose time they guard. My wife has always told me to let these people know how much I appreciate their efforts on my behalf, and I do. Arlyn Avery, Maxine Lowell, Barbara Sevier, Karen O'Neill, Anita Greene, Frank Parisi, and Bobbi Howe.

Finally, this project owes its continued life at HarperBusiness to many different editors who have kept its flame kindled. Martha Jewett and Ed Breslin ferried the project along until it was eventually passed into the able and willing hands of Frank Mount. Frank encouraged and molded this book, believed in it, and was even properly impressed when I needed to feel that support. He has always been genuine, honest, and professional in both disagreement and agreement. Fortunately for me, we agreed far more than we ever disagreed. I should be so lucky to work with other editors who care as much as Frank.

—Ron Schultz
Santa Fe, New Mexico

WHAT OPENS

All light is available light

PAUL STRAND

Even from here, 33 floors up,
through spandrel glass
the city visible but barely seen,
sun suggesting shadows
on the wide mahogany, the desk
polished to reflection.
Suddenly (or did the focus shift?),
the shapes, the telephone, the intercom
break open & what speaks
illuminates, the forms, the shadows
sheer surprise, as though
what waited found its light.

PEGGY AYLSWORTH

INTRODUCTION
BUILDING A
FOUNDATION
FOR DECISIONS

WHAT FACTORS RAISE successful decision makers' abilities above those of others? Are they smarter? Are they more creative, more daring, more confident? What separates them?

It isn't just a matter of having the right information. In that case, everyone could make the right decision. The difference between making the right decision and the wrong one lies not in what is obvious, but in what is subtle and often unseen. What is happening inside these successful decision makers when they have to make a decision?

What prompted Harold Williams's engineering of the Getty–Texaco/Pennzoil takeover, which would later result in the largest legal judgment in corporate history against Texaco? What directed John Sculley to make the foundation-shaking decisions behind his successful restructuring of Apple Computer? How did twenty-seven-year-old Robert Pittman push MTV to the top of the charts and then assume leadership of Time Warner Enterprises? How did Gene Kranz, NASA's director of mission operations, make the final decision to set Neil Armstrong and Buzz Aldrin down—with their on-board computer temporarily malfunctioning—on the moon? When the Committee to Reelect the President tried to persuade Peter Dailey that he did not need an audit of his work on Richard Nixon's 1972 campaign, why did he insist on it—and save himself untold grief when the Watergate scandal unfolded? What source directs Dr. Lewis Goldfrank, chief of the Emergency Services Department at New York's Bellevue Hospital, when he has to decide how to treat an emergency comatose patient with no medical history whose life rests on his decision?

These are a few of the decisions *Unconventional Wisdom* will examine. Each decision is as varied as the personality that made it, yet in each case, the process, that ability to bring together all the necessary elements for decisive action, has an essential common thread: the capacity to recognize the possibilities and then choose the appropriate direction. Digging into how each of these decision makers goes about this visionary and sorting process can be very personal. Don Richard, a former vice-president for Jack Tramiel's Atari Corporation, was at first reluctant to discuss these ideas. He felt it was hitting him in his religion.

This inquiry is exactly my purpose. *Unconventional Wisdom* exposes those inner beliefs and voices that high pressure decision makers listen to, yet rarely share. Why? Because to understand how successful decision makers decide, one must look into those hidden areas they hold as gospel. For many of these people, this process is like religion. These are among their deepest, most private thoughts and feelings. To talk about them is to open themselves in ways they're not usually accustomed.

Nonetheless, it is important to bring these issues to the surface. By acknowledging the process, a number of good things can happen. First, the process can be refined in ways that increase its functioning. Second, it makes decision makers conscious of wider realms of possibilities. Third, opening these inner processes begins to round the individual, allowing for greater use of the power of the whole brain.

What will be presented in the chapters to come is in essence a storybook, filled with real-life stories of today's high pressure decision makers, demonstrating their processes, their leaps, and the decisions they've made.

These are decision makers at the top of their fields, fields that include corporate business, sports, entertainment, government, and the world of medicine. Their experience and approach to decision making offers a unique look inside their various operating worlds and themselves.

They speak about establishing their objectives, setting forth their procedures, and gathering information, which includes knowing how much information they really need. They explain how they know when the time is right—or not right—to strike. They expose the way they sense trends and cycles, the ways of markets and mergers. They talk about motivation, working with their people, and their success. And they reveal throughout it all their deep and continual trust in their well-honed inner capabilities.

It is within this vast realm of inner processes that a decision maker's success lies. At the heart of that source is a function called intuition—the hunch, the gut feeling, or the sudden inspiration. Whatever it is called, out of the over sixty decision makers interviewed for this book, each and every one credited this quiet, often elusive, seemingly irrational intuitive sense for their success. This is not to imply that intuition is the sole guide in making decisions. Nonetheless, as we shall see, when the pressure is turned up, intuition is turned on.

As I will outline later, defining intuition has often been difficult. Since it is primarily an unconscious process, it defies what we regard as rational reasoning. Thinking is rational. One plus one equals two. But intuition is an inner process where information and data are synthesized without the benefit of a calculator or a flow chart. Intuition, according to psychologist Carl Gustav Jung, is an unconscious ability to perceive possibilities, to see the global picture while addressing the local situation.

Learning to hear this inner voice, to recognize its manifestations, to trust its innate sense of direction, and to heed its warnings are the lessons to be found in each of the stories that follow. As will be demonstrated, intuition is the process of knowing what you know. The key to successfully employing this information is to trust the process enough to act on that knowledge.

Tony-award-winning director and artistic director of the Mark Taper Forum in Los Angeles, Gordon Davidson, likens the process to an Olympic high diver on the end of a diving board. "When you leave the board, you're off in space, doing whatever one is trained to do, which is not unlike those moments of making decisions. It's not unrelated to that moment in a play when the lights go down, and then come up and you have to start acting. The actor literally doesn't know whether the words will come out, whether he'll remember his lines, whether anything will be like what he prepared for. That's when you're going on a combination of technique, training, and intuition."

To facilitate the development of the reader's own intuitive process, there is a series of exercises at the end of the book. These activities have been designed and tested to help identify, improve, and unlock intuition, while preparing decision makers to listen to and know what they know. As the famed scientist Louis Pasteur said, "Fortune favors the prepared mind, making it ripe for discovery." And as the late, world-renowned choreographer Martha Graham reiterated, "There's no such thing as the bulb suddenly going on. You must prepare your mind for intuition." *Unconventional Wisdom* is a journey that will prepare its readers to trust their intuition and to open themselves to a world of innovative possibilities.

Understanding the inner workings of a decision maker's process is a complex and often elusive journey. People have been bickering and quibbling over these issues ever since humanity first put its brains to work, deciding if it was truly wise to try and kill that charging beast or if it really made more sense to continue eating berries and roots.

Ultimately, decision making is a matter of what we know. If we know that a charging beast can't see beyond its nose, we can prepare ourselves to meet its charge. What we do is use past knowledge, experience, and values, together with the current situation, our understanding and vision, and apply that to the future.

If this is an acceptable assumption, then knowing how we know offers a framework for better understanding the process of decision making.

During the sixth and seventh centuries B.C., whenever the leaders of ancient Greece were faced with a pressing decision, they hurried off in the direction of Mount Parnassus. Climbing the rugged path, they would come to the Oracle at Delphi. Here, Apollo made his will known to these early decision makers through the hot sulfurous vapors spewing from a fissure in the side of this active volcano.

The Greek philosophers, however, wanted more than readings of vaporous emissions. They wanted to possess and understand the knowledge. Like Prometheus, they wanted to bring the fire of knowledge down to earth.

Thus inspired, philosophers like Plato, Socrates, and Aristotle delved headlong into logic, ethics, and the nature of knowledge. They expressed their discoveries in dialogues and treatises.

For Aristotle, there were two fundamental kinds of knowing. The first was scientific. This was knowledge based on proven fundamental steps. A scientist knew something was true because through experimentation he had a basic understanding of the assumptions upon which his experiment was based.

The second form of knowing for Aristotle was immediate knowledge. This was independent of any kind of experiment because the basic assumptions on which this knowledge was based, ultimate truths, were intangible. Aristotle believed that immediate knowledge was gained through our senses and experience. The image that came from this vision, however, was not of the object being viewed, but of the "universal." For Aristotle, these basic assumptions of the universal could only be induced. This immediate knowledge he called "intuition."

Aristotle concluded that the only kinds of knowledge that were always true were science and intuition. Furthermore, there was no other kind of thought more accurate than science except intuition, because it was only through intuition that the basic assumptions of all knowledge could be understood.

What then is this thing called "intuition"? The English word intuition comes from the Latin *intueri*, "to look on," and is derived from *in*, "on," and *tueri*, "to see," or "to watch." For the Greek philosophers, intuition was an immediate thought or understanding not based on deduction. Furthermore, it was an insight derived without the use of the sense organs, ordinary experience, or in its pure form, reason.

If this seems to be a rather abstract definition, it is. Intuition for the Greeks, and for those that followed, was intricately knotted into metaphysics. It was a way of grasping those first aspects of the world that had no other physical handle for perception. This makes for a pretty abstract stomping ground.

This system of beliefs about how humans hold knowledge basically held true until the seventeenth century, when the revelations of Copernicus, Kepler, Galileo, and Newton revolutionized science. Their astronomical observations shocked the Christian world, which had imposed a philosophical orthodoxy based on scripture. However, the logical, step-by-step process on which scientific knowledge had always been based now showed that the universe was not as had been previously believed. What we thought was "true" was now thrown into turmoil by the words of these scientific heretics.

René Descartes was the first to try and incorporate these scientific discoveries into a new way of explaining the process of how man knows. For his work, Descartes stands as the father of modern philosophy.

Descartes's approach was simple: Doubt everything. He found that the only thing he could not doubt was thought, which brought him to his famous pronouncement: *Cogito ergo sum* (I think therefore I am.). This in turn led to his general principle: "All things that we conceive very clearly and very distinctly are true." According to Descartes, we made these distinctions by approaching problems systematically, and analyzing them piece by piece. This meant moving from the simple to the more complex while reviewing everything thoroughly to make sure nothing was omitted.

It was by following this painstakingly scientific process that Descartes came to his proposition that thought was truth. With one powerful philosophic thrust, Descartes separated the mind and body. They were now two separate entities. This realization freed philosophy from having to reconcile the metaphysical with the physical. All human thoughts, according to Descartes, were applicable to the laws of physics and therefore science. After Descartes, logic and reason towered over the more immediate and seemingly unreasoned intuitive knowledge.

Having divorced metaphysics, philosophers then turned away from the epistemological question of how humans know, to redirect their focus toward human existence.

The process of trying to unravel the inner workings of knowledge did not stop here. Psychology soon picked up the inquiry. At the forefront of this redivision of the study of the mind were the dynamic psychologists. The most influential of these were Sigmund Freud and Carl Jung. After three thousand years of debate, the mind had its own science.

The development of modern analytic psychology began in earnest to discover what philosophy had only conjectured. Though influenced by philosophical ideals, the psychoanalytic process was an attempt to scientifically understand and explain the roots of man's inner processing. The path did not begin at Freud's doorstep, but it certainly wasn't far away.

Freud's primary emphasis was on mental disturbances or psychopathology. Freud's concern was how inner human nature, such as desires, complexes, and fears, got in the way of functioning in the outer world. The outer life for Freud was humanity's attempt to satisfy the needs of those inner realms. The process of unraveling these hidden levels was, of course, psychoanalysis.

Prior to Freud, the interplay between feelings, perceptions, thought processes, and willpower was long considered to be conscious. Freud placed them squarely in the unconscious, saying it was only from the passing of this unconscious material into consciousness that individuals had any idea of their existence. This required a close look at these unconscious transferences to clearly understand human behavior.

For the most part, Freud directed his inner-world examinations at the troubled mind seeking satisfaction. He was not concerned with what might be loosely called the "well" mind or how someone might utilize the functioning mind to act and make decisions normally in the world. That was not of interest to Freud. He was, after all, a medical doctor. His focus was on healing sick people. The way to accomplish this was to discover what it was that prevented people from functioning well.

Carl Jung viewed it a bit differently. Jung saw the human mind as a whole of many parts struggling for completion. There was sickness and there was wellness. Knowledge and reality were for Jung matters of consciousness, not illness. Jung often said that one of his greatest debts to Freud was that Freud explored psychopathology so exhaustively that it left Jung free to explore health and its limitless possibilities.

Like Freud, Jung had a medical education. In addition, German and Eastern philosophy greatly influenced him.

Jung addressed head on the process of relating to the world, gathering knowledge, and committing it to action. According to Jung, people are either extraverted or introverted. Extraverts direct their energy toward the outer world while introverts direct theirs primarily inward, the split between the two being about fifty-fifty.

In addition to these two fundamental attitudes, Jung also believed there were four basic functions of the mind: thinking, feeling, sensation, and intuition. This division follows fairly closely along classical philosophic lines. Where it differs is in the dynamic application of these four functions.

Jung can best describe this division, which researchers now call "Jung's Typology." "First of all we have sensation, our sense function," Jung stated in a lecture he gave at the Tavistock Clinic in London, England, in 1935. "Sensation tells me that something is: It does not tell what it is and it does not tell me other things about that something; it only tells me that something is.

"The next function is thinking. Thinking, if you ask a philosopher," Jung noted, tongue in cheek, "is something very difficult, so never ask a philosopher about it because he is the only man who does not know what thinking is. Everybody else knows what thinking is. When you say to a man, 'Now think properly,' he knows exactly what you mean, but a philosopher never knows. Thinking in its simplest tells us what a thing is. It gives a name to a thing.

"The third function is feeling. Here minds become very confused and people get very angry when I speak about feeling, because according to their view I say something dreadful about it. Feeling informs you through its feeling-tones of the values of things. Feeling tells you for instance whether a thing is acceptable or agreeable or not. It tells you what a thing is worth to you."

Jung then summed up. "Sensation tells us that a thing is. Thinking tells us what that thing is, feeling tells us what it is worth. Now what else could there be? There is another category and that is time. Things have a past and they have a future. They come from somewhere and they go to somewhere, and you can't see where they come from, and you cannot know where they go to, but you get what the Americans call a hunch. That is what is called intuition."

Jung went on to describe intuition as an openness to possibilities, an ability to envision in a single picture the whole. Defined in this way, intuition combines both the philosophies of Immanuel Kant and Henri Bergson with one added step. Like Kant's ideas, intuition was a knowing that synthesized both prior knowledge and present. Like Bergson, it revealed a total image. However, Jung felt intuition was not only a metaphysical manifestation but also an active process, a way of perceiving in the physical world.

According to Jung, the ideal situation would be to have a balance among the four functions. That is nearly impossible. The difficulty many people have in recognizing their feelings points out some of the problems, and when intuition comes into play—probably the least understood and definitely the most abstract of the functions—the situation gets even tougher.

One difficulty in comprehending the scope of intuition is that by Jung's definition, it is not three dimensional, but four dimensional. Albert Einstein's indirect contribution to psychology established that we live in a physical universe dominated by four dimensions: height, width, depth, and time. Because the universe is constantly changing, everything carries the final measure of where it occurs in time. Unlike its three sibling dimensions, time is difficult to envision. So too is its mind counterpart, intuition.

There are some people, though, who are quite comfortable in this fluid intuitive realm, especially when it comes to making decisions, just as there are some people who swear that the only way to answer a problem is to think it through completely. The reason for this, according to Jung, is that each of these functions has its polar opposite. Thinking's opposite is feeling, and intuition's opposite is sensation. Jung thought most people had one or two developed functions, the other two being relatively undeveloped. So, if someone is a thinking type, it would be said that their feeling function was then inferior or undeveloped. The case is the same with intuition and its opposite sensation.

For Jung, intuition and sensation are the functions that perceive situations. Sensation tries to reach the most accurate perception of what is, while intuition tries to encompass the greatest possibilities. When John Wayne went after the bad guy, his decision making was immediate. There was no reflection on anything other than his perception of a pressing concern. To that end he was completely directed. Time stood still: the height of sensation. By way of contrast, when Luke Skywalker left to become a Jedi warrior, to learn to listen to the Force, his direction was on the larger picture, and very intuitive.

It is important to note that psychological typing is not an exact science and that its classifications are not rigid pigeon holes to lock a specific type in forever. They are intended to be used more like guide posts on a surveyor's map; the hills and valleys are all noted, but there are lots of uncharted areas. There are a number of tests devised to discover the psychological type of an individual. The Myers-Briggs Type Indicator was devised by lay professionals Isabel Briggs Myers and Peter Myers in the 1970s and has gained broad popular acceptance. One of the very first typological tests, and one still widely in use today, is the Gray-Wheelwright Test. Three colleagues of Jung's developed this test: Horace Gray, and Joseph and Jane Wheelwright. I have included a copy of the test in chapter 14. As mentioned above, all these tests should be viewed as merely indications of a person's strengths and weaknesses.

Jung's four functions are a direct descendant from the Greek philosophers' impression, although Jung, like Freud, separated the conscious mind from the unconscious. But unlike Freud, Jung separates feeling from sensation and brings back the notion of intuition. As an extension of Greek thought, Jung sees intuition as perceiving data in the unconscious mind and then delivering its answer whole and complete. It's the light bulb going on, which can startle those unaccustomed to its force.

"I am convinced," says psychologist Rollo May in *The Courage to Create*, "that this (illumination) is the usual accompaniment of the breakthrough of unconscious experience into consciousness. Here is again part of the reason the experience scares us so much: The world, both inwardly and outwardly, takes on an intensity that may be overwhelming." The unity of the unconscious experience with the conscious is a dynamic and immediate fusion. As described by Dr. May, it is a time when the world becomes vivid and unforgettable.

But, as Dr. Joseph Wheelwright, codeveloper of the Gray-Wheelwright Jungian Type Survey, is quick to caution, intuition also has its negative side. The intuitive person is often the one "tripping over the hearth rug, because he doesn't know where the hell he's going," says Wheelwright, an intuitive type himself. "Well, he may know where he's going," he continues, "but it may not have anything to do with his feet. The sensation type never forgets his feet."

Dr. Murray Gell-Mann, the Nobel physicist who proposed and

named the quark theory (as the fundamental particle of matter) and one of the few scientists willing to acknowledge what has come to be called the "irrational," has said, "There are a lot of mental processes out of awareness different from rational thought processes. I think this is the most important part of human psychology. But just because one is interested in unconscious mental processes or the irrational, one doesn't have to accept the word of every Tom, Dick, Sigmund, and Carl about how they function. Although they hold a lot of truths, Freud and Jung were rather unscientific in their approaches. Our understanding of the irrational aspect of human behavior would be better enhanced if the unconscious processes were studied scientifically." His thinking takes us directly to the emergence of the physical study of the human brain.

Today, our understanding of the brain is light-years ahead of what we knew during the first half of the century. In the 1960s, Dr. Roger Sperry and Dr. Michael Gazzaniga experimented with split brain operations to treat epilepsy. They discovered that the brain is actually composed of two brains, the right and left. The left generally controls the majority of conscious aspects, including logic and the essential Broca's area, which controls verbalization and language. This is named for the French scientist Paul Broca, who first identified it. The right brain generally handles those areas that are literally difficult to put into words, one being intuition. In order for the right brain to communicate its process, it has to transfer its impulses to the left brain. It does this through images and sometimes even dreams.

The development of psychology and the recent findings on the workings of the brain say quite a bit about how people know and the way people make decisions. During the nineteenth century, the overpowering philosophical viewpoints of the rationalists, empiricists, and pragmatists, which saw the world as certain, predominated. The prevailing worldview metaphor for this mechanistic universe was a machine—the parts make the whole. The romantics had an effect by embracing the "irrational" functions of the world, greatly influencing psychology. But it was not until the abominable destruction of modernity that the "irrational" functions gained a strong foothold in the modern world.

Where once thought and reason had made perfect sense in a certain world, the new uncertainty of existence threw that model asunder. This realization of uncertainty made intuition an integral part of the process again, as Jung had suggested. As Kant pointed out, intuition was a way to know when things were uncertain.

There were still other factors that pushed thought away from certainty and toward the intuitive. One aspect of Heisenberg's uncertainty principle basically states that the act of measurement affects the thing measured, making it virtually impossible to know everything about an object. By applying that principle to the nature of our quantum universe, uncertainty becomes a driving force. The impact of these ideas has only just begun to change the current world view from its formerly separatist and mechanistic perspective to one based much more on the relationship of one thing to another.

Another factor that has directed us away from the highly rational certainty concepts is the computer, originally the ultimate product of reason. With the computer came a rapid growth in available information and, conversely, a decline in the amount of time that was available to people to analyze this information. The other issue, which was directly related to and in fact caused that lack of time, was the dramatic shift in the world competitive marketplace.

Where corporations once had a seven-year economic cycle within which to plan their strategies, change has become the rule. Not only have there been near disastrous shifts in the American economy, but the emergence of the global marketplace has put added pressure to produce faster and with better quality. This uncertainty made old methods involving laborious, time-consuming analysis before major capital expenditures obsolete. Something had to change.

What happened was a growing trend toward intuitive decision making. A number of studies that began to surface in the late

1970s and 1980s reflected this trend—in all competitive areas of life. They also demonstrated that in a world filled with uncertain outcomes, those that best utilized this intuitive function were often the most successful.

In the early 1960s, Douglas Dean and John Mihalasky began a ten-year study called the PSI Communications Project at the Newark College of Engineering. Psi is the twenty-third letter of the Greek alphabet and the first syllable of such words as psychology, psychiatry, etc. For Dean and Mihalasky, psi was an attempt to scientifically explore the realms of what was commonly referred to as ESP. Since they were unsure whether this phenomenon was either sensory or a perception, they stuck with the label of psi.

In one of their tests, Dean and Mihalasky tested sixty-seven company presidents for their psi abilities. After the test, they then asked these presidents to supply certain financial information about their companies. Out of those that replied, 60 percent had doubled their real profits in the past five years. In checking the scores of those presidents, each one of them had scored higher on the psi test than average. The 40 percent who had not doubled their profits all scored lower than average.

Not yet satisfied, Dean and Mihalasky conducted their test again with another group of company presidents. The results were the same. Those presidents with companies that had doubled their profits over the past five years all had higher than average psi scores. Of those tested who had not doubled their profits, 60 percent scored below average, while the other 40 percent all ran companies that had improved profits by 51 to 100 percent.

Dean and Mihalasky's results do not necessarily prove that profit making and intuitive ability are related, but, as they saw it, "they (the test results) indicate that the probability of getting a superior profit maker is enhanced by choosing a man who scores well."

A more recent study, specifically aimed at intuitive management, tested more than 2,500 managers employed at a variety of different levels in both the private and public sectors. The study was put together by Weston Agor, director of the Master of Public Administration Program at the University of Texas at El Paso.

Agor used a combination of the Myers-Briggs Type Indicator test and sections of a test called the Mobius Psi-Q test.

The test comprised two parts. First, it measured the management style of the individual, testing for whether the manager was primarily right-brain oriented, left-brain oriented, or integrated. This section was based on the Mobius Psi-Q test. The second part addressed the individual's "underlying ability to use intuition to make management decisions," and was based on the Myers-Briggs test.

Weston's findings were dramatic. They showed, according to his analysis of the data, that "intuition appears to be a skill that is more prevalent as one moves up the management ladder." He found that top managers, in every group, tested significantly higher than middle and lower management in their underlying ability to use intuition to make decisions. His study also showed that top executives integrated their intuitive abilities well with their other functions, but concluded that when top executives were ready to act, they appeared to rely more often than not on intuition as their guide.

What the integration factor says about typology is that when all functions are well-utilized, performance is enhanced. If a four-cylinder car is running on only three cylinders, it is not running efficiently. Agor's study pointed out that intuition, which since Descartes had been considered to be both unreasonable and unscientific (especially in a very reasonable and certain world), has now returned to a place of prominence in the decision-making process.

Studies like those conducted by Agor, Dean and Mihalasky, David Lowe of the Institute for Future Forecasting, Arthur Reber of Brooklyn College, and Daniel Isenberg of the *Harvard Business Review*, all confirm this shift.

Like Agor, Isenberg's work found that business as usual was not business as one might expect. He spent two years studying the thought processes used by dozens of senior managers. These men ranged in age from their low forties to their upper fifties. All had ten to thirty years of managerial experience. The companies they worked for were in a variety of businesses, from high-tech to low, and all were responsible for the overall performance of their companies. Isenberg found that "Senior managers seldom think in ways that one might simplistically view as 'rational.'" Instead, whenever stakes were high, the situation unfamiliar or the problem tangled, intuition was the tool most likely used to unravel the problem.

Isenberg's stated aim was to help relieve managers of the discrepancy between how they were "supposed to" think, and how they really processed information. Isenberg found that the majority of managers favored the intuitive over the more analytic approaches, though most believed it was not how things were normally done.

Few philosophers, psychologists, or scientists would question the fact that mankind has entered an increasingly uncertain era. In spite of this uncertainty, the once powerful dominance of the Cartesian, empiricist, rationalist, and pragmatic points of view can still be seen today. It can be seen in those who are still reluctant to trust inner processes and functions, such as intuition. It could be that this denial is actually their last grasp at what was once a certain world.

Nonetheless, a shift in how decision makers process information is definitely underway. By putting all these elements together—the philosophical, the psychological, the physiological, and now the economic—a new and powerful pattern of action seems to be clearly emerging. The intuitive function of the mind plays a vital role in the process of how a human being knows, and, therefore, how he or she decides to act in the world. But it has also been shown that it is not intuition alone that gets the job done. It is a combination of experience, knowledge, thoughtful analysis, value, as well as the ability to view the big picture, which intuition draws on and works from. The integration of these inner processes is the foundation upon which a decision maker can build his success. Intuition in a vacuum is a vacuum, or as the executive director of the ACLU, Ira Glasser, says later, "Garbage in, garbage out."

American decision makers are finally coming to accept uncertainty in the world. They have discovered that pure logic and reason could not address the quantity of uncertainty they encountered. Without abandoning logic and reason, they have returned to the only quality that can master uncertainty, intuition. Intuition has, quite simply, filled a pressing need. It has become a tool to meet the current demand of functioning under uncertain conditions. What successful decision makers are saying is that they don't leave home without it.

JOHN SCULLEY

DESIGNING A BETTER APPLE

We asked the captain what course of action he proposed to take toward a beast so large, terrifying, and unpredictable. He hesitated to answer, and then said judiciously: "I think I shall praise it."

ROBERT HASS, *PRAISE*

WHEN APPLE COMPUTER'S Steven Jobs lured John Sculley away from PepsiCo, he is reported to have asked him: "Do you want to spend the rest of your life selling sugar water to kids or do you want to change the world?" It's safe to say that Jobs had little idea how radically Sculley would change Jobs's own personal world, let alone Apple's. Let's just say that Sculley took the Apple challenge. He ran operations and production for a little over two years before he formulated the ouster of Jobs himself. Then, with a clean line and directed managerial style, he propelled Apple back into the forefront of computer sales.

Sculley's vigorous assault on the computer world began with that first decision. At age forty-four, he was already president of Pepsi, and had been guiding that concern quite profitably for five years. When offered the post at Apple, in keeping with Sculley's own philosophy that people in this technological age will change careers three or four times during their worklife, he took the plunge. In the beginning, he stayed out of the public eye, but that would change less than a year after taking over Apple's helm. The groundwork was actually laid a few months before the 1984 Super Bowl.

The board of directors assembled in the screening room. So did the advertising executives, Apple's marketing director, Sculley, and Jobs. The lights went out and a tape machine came on. Stark, eerie images smacking of Orwell's *1984* appeared. Rows of people with shaved heads sat like zombies before an altar-like screen. The dialogue and music matched the mood. Then a female figure carrying a large sledgehammer rushed on, closely pursed by menacing, jack-booted troops. Swinging the hammer over her head, she let it fly, shattering the giant screen filled with the image of Big Brother. It revealed Apple's newest computer, the Macintosh.

The tape machine was turned off. Sculley and Jobs could sense this was it. They looked around at the faces of the board members. As Sculley would later recall, "They just about cried in panic. They couldn't believe we wanted to run it, but they didn't supersede us. They said 'It's your decision, but we think it's terrible.' I sat down with Steve and Mike Murray, the marketing director, and asked, 'Should we do it or not?'"

How is a decision like this made? Were there charts to consult, graphs, any marketing analysis? No. According to Sculley, they based their decision on intuition.

Apple ran that Macintosh commercial, produced by Chiat/Day, only once. It was aired in the middle of the Super Bowl, during the Los Angeles Raiders' dismantling of the Washington Redskins. The effect of Sculley and Jobs's decision was felt almost immediately. When the cameras returned to the game, the announcers on the air paused. They had never seen anything like it. "By the end of the game," Sculley said with a slight smile, "they said the only exciting thing in the Super Bowl that year was the Apple commercial." Though Raider fans may disagree, the next day proved that assessment right. Every news program in the country, beginning with the morning news, ran the commercial, and they kept running it for a week and a half.

"We don't know the exact value of the free media we got," adds Sculley, "but it was probably in excess of ten million dollars, with another ten to fifteen million dollars in free publicity for the project." Almost a decade later, the Macintosh technology remains the core of Apple's production.

"I tend to approach decision making from the right side of the brain," Sculley said from his computer-packed, glass-enclosed, third floor office. A view of the Santa Cruz mountains framed the blue sky in the background. "It's very intuitive. Just like a sailor can sniff the air and knows when a storm is coming up, I have always been good at sniffing the air and knowing when the time is right to make a course correction, or when to make a big investment."

One such enlightened breeze floated Sculley's way just prior to the Macintosh introduction when Apple sales were very soft and IBM had recently unveiled the PC Junior. "I decided that was the time to make a heavy investment," said Sculley, "when most pundits in the industry were saying it was all over, IBM had won, and that Apple's best days were behind us. We went out and committed hundreds of millions of dollars into inventory, dropped our prices by a total of about forty million dollars, and put in very aggressive marketing funds. The goal was simple. I didn't think anybody would want to buy a brand new innovative computer from a company perceived as not doing well. As it turned out, it worked. The momentum turned around dramatically. We doubled the amount of Apple II's we had ever sold in December, and we went into the introduction of the Macintosh riding a wave of momentum.

"All the facts could probably be articulated specifically, but there were a lot of other people who had the same facts but interpreted them differently. The rational approach would have focused on the risks looking too high in that month or in that quarter. I think the more perceptual person would say, wait a minute, none of that will mean anything unless you come out the other end as a winner."

Sculley's confidence in himself and in his intuitive process, his ability to see the big picture and focus on the short-term, are some of the qualities that raise an intuitive decision maker above those stuck in the purely operational analytical approach.

This does not imply that analysis is to be ignored. Having the right data is essential in today's marketplace. Sculley likens it to cooking a good soup. You know your ingredients. You taste it, sniff it, but your experience tells you to let it simmer a while. And like a good cook, you listen to your experience, because you know when it's just right.

Another well-known decision maker, Lee Iacocca, would agree with Sculley. The danger Iacocca points out is trying to make decisions based on 100 percent of the facts. "You never get all the facts," Iacocca says. "If you wait, by the time you do get them, your facts will be out of date, because the market has moved on. ... At some point, you have to take the leap of faith ... because even the right decision is wrong if it's made too late." Good information is *not* like good wine. It does not age well.

If prompt action is the key, how does a decision maker like Sculley avoid the problems of constantly being in a reactive mode, spending time continually fighting fires? The answer is planning.

A wise person once said, "Plans are nothing, but planning is everything!" It is extraordinarily important to do the planning. Not nearly as important is adhering strictly to those plans. What planning does is give you a context for short-term decisions, with a view of the long-term goal, but without a rigid structure that won't allow it to be modified or adjusted.

Goals and planning are what Sculley calls his "architecture." "The most important thing to me," he says, "is to have a clear framework for architecture. What is the destination, and what is the architecture of how we are going to get there?

"Therefore, in planning a strategy, it has to be looked at in terms of what the mission we have as a company is, and then how we will accomplish that in a very dynamic, changing environment where we can't predict when our competitors will make certain moves, or we can't predict changes in consumer trends. It is even more true in this industry where history is not something you can project from, only something you can learn from."

Sculley's friend Regis McKenna, one of the country's first and leading high-tech marketing consultants and the man credited with creating the image of the Silicon Valley, concurs. "A decision is process. People are successful in today's high-tech world by constantly altering and adjusting to the environment. It's a constant process of change. You can't make decisions that are absolute, because there is no absolute. There are only relative situations."

For Sculley, the planning process begins by establishing his goals and creating what he sees as the ideal situation, assuming he could have control over the external environment. He visualizes where it is he wants the company to end up. His strategic decisions grow from that point.

"It's like sailing a boat," he says. "There are certain principles you have to follow. The boat just doesn't sail. Once you're actually out in the weather, among the currents, you trim the sails; you're feeling how it's taking to the wind. It's the same with a business. You get an intuitive feeling of when things are working. If the wind changes, I can change strategies if necessary, but it doesn't mean I've changed destination. It just means I've changed how I'm going to get there."

Decisions are made by Sculley only after addressing the implications of the decision according to the planned mission. Then he makes sure he has correctly identified what the problem actually is. He has found that people tend to rush decisions by trying to decide between options that may not address the real problem.

One quality that has aided Sculley in his corporate endeavors has been his ability to move back and forth between the analytical and the intuitive. He is able to absorb a lot of data and then hold those facts in his head. He allows simmering to take place, checking in every once in a while. He then talks to more people and gets new perspectives, adding their insights into the mixture.

"I can spend hours pouring over numbers and working through prophesies," Sculley says. "In fact, a lot of the prophesies [forecasts] which Pepsi uses to track its market share and sales performance through some twenty-two distribution channels and a million accounts a week were ones I designed in the seventies. But I don't enjoy that side of it nearly as much as I enjoy the more creative side. The reason I was more interested in architecture than painting was that architecture has a certain set of rules. If you violate those rules the building falls down. I like to be creative within the constraints of some structure. I talk in terms of architecture and systems, trying to find visions in terms of what the building blocks are. Most people are talking about return of assets employed, the kind of cash flow returned on investment, and quarterly earnings. Obviously, I have to be accountable for those things or I wouldn't be where I am, but being able to think at the architectural level gives me a structure to be confident in my intuition."

It is Sculley's belief that all great marketing decisions are made by intuition. Experience, data, and a variety of perspectives feed his intuition, and his sense of destination directs it.

It was just this sense that directed Sculley on that late May morning when he headed off a power takeover challenge from the man who brought him into the organization, cofounder and Chairman of the Board Steven Jobs. Exposing Jobs's machinations, Sculley took firm control of the company. He immediately instituted a restructuring plan, consolidating Apple's gangly operations into three distinct functional areas. It was one of the most stressful, wrenching periods any executive can face. Sculley combined engineering, manufacturing, and distribution of all products under one roof. He also established one product development division and one marketing and sales unit.

Sculley seems to be able to find the right, though not necessarily easy, answers. "I believe in the fact that there are windows of opportunity. When the window is open, you go right through it. But when the window is closed, there is no point." Obviously such a moment occurred two weeks after Jobs's departure. At that time, he closed three of Apple's six plants and laid off twelve hundred people.

This was a drastic move, especially in light of Apple's strong, people-oriented culture. Sculley knew, though, that if the organism as a whole was going to survive, Apple's operations had to be pruned back. This was not solely a pragmatic decision, even though it was characterized by John Matlock, president of Info-Corp, a Silicon Valley market research firm, as Sculley's attempt to change Apple "from a religion into a business." It was Matlock's opinion that "when you've got cold calculating competitors like IBM, you can't beat them with voodoo."

What Sculley used was far from voodoo. It was what he called his "operational perspective," a combination of self-confidence, an awareness through experience of his mistakes, and an ability to go back and forth between his big picture, global perspective, and the details. It is this sense that Sculley credits for knowing when to cut his losses. And truly in this case, Apple was cutting its losses. It was a day considered by some to be the most difficult day in Apple's history. But the record books also show that it was Sculley's taking firm control of Apple's rudder that eventually turned Apple around.

Even Steven Jobs's admirers had to admit that Sculley's decisions were the best for Apple. Apple cofounder Steven Wozniac liked what he saw, too. Two months after Jobs resigned, Wozniac bought back $5 million of Apple stock, with plans to buy another $15 million more. The market also agreed with Sculley. Apple stock has risen from a low point close to $14 a share to a 1992 high of $70.

"In this industry," Sculley says, "which is a brand new industry, where the technology is changing, the competition is changing, markets are being created, other markets are being saturated, it's just about impossible to use history to project from. You can only use history to learn from. Therefore, the whole decision making process tends to be a lot more dynamic than you would find in a traditional business. You can't fall back on tried and true ways. You have to continually be testing and retesting the validity of your thinking and your strategy as you move forward."

Apple's future hung in a precarious balance. Sculley could see the direction the computer industry was headed over the next couple of years. He knew who his competition was. He also knew that the computer world was still emerging and that even IBM didn't have all the answers. "In a business that is just starting to take shape," he said, "I think the intuitive style of management is a lot more important because the variables are so uncertain."

To make a decision that not only affects the lives of twelve hundred people but the whole culture of a business is a bold move. Sculley had his business analysis, his figures were accounted for, but a decision like this had to have something more. Sculley had to be able to move easily between his two spheres, the more abstract and the more pragmatic. He had to ask questions both about what Apple was trying to build and how they were going to get where they wanted to go. The computer industry, though, had its own special problems. Sculley couldn't call on the same kinds of specific data that traditional companies could amass. He had to have faith and trust in another kind of data processing.

One area Sculley has been able to avoid successfully with his decisions is what author Arthur C. Clarke refers to as the "failure of nerve" or the "failure of imagination." A failure of nerve occurs when, to quote Clarke, "given all the relevant facts, the would-be prophet cannot see that they point out an inescapable conclusion." The catch phrase of these nerveless failures is "they said it couldn't be done." An 1865 editorial in the *Boston Globe* exemplifies this problem. It appeared after the arrest of Joshua Coopersmith for trying to raise funds to create a device called a telephone. "Well informed people know it is impossible to transmit the voice over wires and that were it possible to do so, the thing would be of no practical use." Sculley has never been one to exhibit a failure of nerve.

▪ ▪ ▪

Beginning in 1990, Sculley and Apple Computers made a couple of fearless moves. First, Sculley turned over the daily responsibility for Apple's existing products to the company's chief operating officer, Michael Spindler. He did this so he could concentrate on pushing Apple into new areas. As he declared in an article in the *Wall Street Journal*, "We have a new agenda. The vision is the same—empowering individuals. But we're expanding that vision to a lot of other emerging markets."

Shortly after this move, Apple began shipping the low-priced Macintosh Classic and LC models. A year later, Sculley followed that major market adjustment with the introduction of Apple's PowerBook notebooks. Both decisions were great successes. By lowering prices Sculley was able to increase Apple's PC market-share by 8 percent in one year.

Then in July 1991 Sculley shocked the computer world by forging an agreement with arch rival IBM to form a partnership to be known as Taligent. He realized that in order for Apple to break into the corporate market and establish itself outside of the personal computer world, Apple had to make some major alliances. Sculley went to IBM and took the intuitive leap. "We decided to show IBM our best stuff." This consisted of a new generation of computer software Apple had poured a great deal of money into, which Sculley had code-named "Pink." Sculley's trusted intuitive process proved to be right. IBM was tickled by "Pink" and the partnership was formed.

Sculley knew this alliance was risky business, but he felt the opportunity was essential for Apple's growth. By maintaining their proprietary stance, marketshares would eventually begin to shrink. As one trusted Sculley battle general explained it, "You have to take a leap of faith that you'll end up with access to a bigger market." For Sculley and Apple, the leap was the right one.

"When you design high-technology products," he said, "people can't articulate what product they ought to build because they have no reference point. It comes down to finding a group of people that share the same values, who have a passion for great products, so that you can trust their instincts as well as your own. It has to go beyond the monetary sense. It has got to be in terms of how are we going to create something that hasn't been done before? In many cases we aren't only creating new products but new markets. So, I would say the words 'faith and trust' are far more important in this kind of business than the world I came from at Pepsi."

Sculley's vision to create new markets became reality in the first months of 1992 when he announced dramatic plans for Apple's diversification. Sculley had once again reshaped and redefined Apple's architecture. It was no longer going to be just a manufacturer of personal computers but a global electronics corporation, with multiple businesses and partners. Sculley's plan was to build and sell consumer electronics, telecommunications devices, and computers. If Sculley pulled this off, one Japanese consultant believed that there might very well be a little apple on every consumer electronic product being made in the world.

Sculley inaugurated this new vision by introducing a new class of products called Personal Digital Assistants. These devices were described as very portable, easy-to-use, specifically designed computers that have advanced communication capabilities and the ability to display and manipulate text, sound, and images.

Apple's prototype for these PDAs was code-named Newton. Newton is a pen-based computer that recognizes handwriting and can maintain general information, including a calendar, as well as dial phone numbers and send faxes, all in a format smaller than a letter-sized notepad.

At the same time these new ideas were being introduced to an awestruck market, Sculley continued to make alliances with companies like Sony, IBM, and Sharp so that the work of producing these products could be handed over to others, with Apple collecting the royalties. The turn of the millennium prospects for Apple's computers, telecommunications, consumer electronics, electronic media, and publishing concerns are tremendous. Sculley has described this incredibly ambitious plan as taking a leap from "the sandbox to the beach."

Corporate ambitions succeed when the market is ripe and their people can deliver. If being willing and able to have faith and trust that those around you will deliver what you ask are qualities of leadership, Sculley has definitely been Apple's leader. As he says and his actions make clear, "Leadership starts with having a very clear vision of where you are going. You must also have the ability to articulate that vision so people can understand the structure of where you are going. Leadership is not individual. It means getting things done through teamwork. Personally, I have always been much more interested in leadership than management."

Developing that sense of direction, that context for decisions making, is the key for Sculley. "I spend a lot of time making sure I'm correctly defining what the problem is and that I have the proper vantage point to obtain the right perspective. Alan Kay [a computer theorist and system designer]," Sculley continues, "made a very insightful comment. He maintains, 'Point of view is worth 80 IQ points.' If you have the right perspective you can be a lot smarter." Sculley spends a great deal of time considering his vantage point and making sure he has correctly defined the problem.

"A lot of people put their energy into the decision itself. They don't put enough energy into figuring out whether the problem is correct, if their destination is correct, or if their vantage point is correct. Instead, they worry about whether their decision is correct without having a frame of reference. I think intuition requires a firm grasp of that frame of reference."

A group of people waiting to escort Sculley to a presentation gathered outside his glass office. They anxiously looked at their watches. Sculley smiled and held up one finger. "I think people who do manage intuitively," he continued, once again undistracted, "find it a pretty comfortable thing. I have been in very high-stress industries, and yet I don't feel much stress. I think a lot of it is I don't stay awake at night worrying about decisions. If I worry about something, I worry about whether or not we have thought through correctly where the world will be in three or four years, not about the decision I'm making today."

Under Sculley's leadership, Apple Computer's evolution has proceeded profitably. He has been able to maintain both Apple's culture and its business. He's accomplished this by trusting his own inner process in the most heated of times. His decisions are confident and direct. He has gathered the facts, placed them in the correct perspective, and then let the process go. In so doing, Sculley has positioned Apple Computer as a world competitor for the year 2000 and beyond. Having done that, in June 1993 Sculley resigned as CEO of Apple. He felt it was time to pursue a new direction, to spend more time with his family and to think about the future.

2

ROBERTA WILLIAMS

FAIRYTALES CAN COME TRUE

Some things have to be believed to be seen.

RALPH HODGSON

SHIPWRECKED ON THE shores of a mysterious island chain, you launch your odyssey across strange and wondrous lands, encountering such weird and terrifying creatures as the Five Gnomes of the Senses and the Winged Ones. Finally, you must confront and defeat the Lord of the Dead. If that's not your idea of fun, maybe you'd prefer to die thirty-nine different ways amid scorching deserts, along sheer mountain cliffs, and in eerie, bedeviled dark forests as you try to help King Graham rescue his family from the evil wizard, Mordack. Is adventure your game? Is fantasy your bailiwick? Are you enchanted by witches, wizards, and fairies of unearthly strength? Roberta Williams was and is, and on the strength and power of her vision, she and her husband Ken have built a $57 million company, starting from their kitchen table.

This is no fairytale. In creating Sierra On-Line, Roberta Williams created an industry—the 3-D animated computer adventure game. At thirty-seven, Williams has written, designed, and sold more home computer games than any other person in computer game history. Her achievements in this field, like her games, are legendary.

When her husband, eager to create a FORTRAN compiler for Apple computers, brought an Apple II into their Simi Valley, California, home, his twenty-seven-year-old wife was not pleased. "That little machine represented several mortgage payments for the house we someday wanted to own," she recalls. Her concerns, however, would soon be alleviated. Ken, anticipating his wife's reaction, also brought her one of the original text adventure games.

When she finished the game she was incredibly disappointed, so she mapped out a game of her own. She then dropped the pile of puzzles and maps she had concocted on the kitchen table before her husband and told him to get busy encoding the game. Bored by the lack of visuals in the text game, she challenged him to figure out how to include pictures. When they were done, the Williamses had created Mystery House, the world's first graphic adventure game.

Ten months and fifteen thousand copies later, On-Line Systems, soon to become Sierra On-Line, moved from the Williams's kitchen to offices in Coarsegold, California, in the Sierra Nevada foothills. Today they employ more than 550 people at three different locations and have grown to be the world's leading computer entertainment software company. Their success is due in large part to the extremely fertile imagination of Roberta Williams.

But then she always felt she was different, apart from other people. "As if I was somehow removed, and I never understood why," she says as she reflects on her own motivations. "My daydreams of myself were normally on a grandiose scale. I was always among riches or saving other people from peril." Which, of course, is incredibly helpful to a woman who would one day translate those visions into fabulously successful computer adventure games.

The adventure, however, has been played out on grounds other than computer screens. Sierra On-Line has had to battle for its success at every step. It has been a battle, too, for Williams to assume her voice in the business. But like her games, she has found the way to emerge victorious—through a combination of intuition and common sense. She follows this course whenever a company decision must be made, and there have been many in the rise and fall and resurrection of Sierra. The moral of the tale is for the princess to be heard, she must speak up.

Two years after the Williamses had begun their meteoric climb, it was decided that in order to take Sierra On-Line to its next level, some new, uncharted territory had to be explored. Williams's husband felt that to maintain their distance on the competition and continue selling product, it was essential for them to bring in some venture capital.

In 1981 a venture capital concern offered the Williamses $1 million in return for a small piece of equity. Ken thought it was just what they needed to improve their collective vision. Roberta sensed something else from the start, especially about the woman representing the venture capitalists, but she couldn't articulate the feeling. "I went out to lunch with her," Roberta recalls, "and she was very business-like, very official sounding, and I remember being very uncomfortable with her and the situation."

Williams was only twenty-eight at the time and not very worldly when it came to the pluses and minuses of a large-scale business/money decision. All she knew was that she didn't feel comfortable with it. Ken, age twenty-seven and still a business rookie, was sold. They flew to Boston to meet with the principals of the company. Roberta remembers repeating her warning, "I don't like this. Let's not do it." But they proceeded. That decision would ultimately trigger a downward cycle at Sierra that very nearly crushed its business.

Had Williams trusted her intuition, they might have avoided the problems that would follow. It's fairly easy to not trust the intuitive feeling when a person's self-confidence in certain areas is low or other pressures outweigh the unspecified impulses rising from within. The consequences, however, can be devastating to an organization when a leader goes against what they know. This was certainly the case at Sierra.

The money was barely warm in the vault before Sierra's new partners established Sierra's board of directors—three members from Sierra and three from the venture capitalists.

As Roberta had feared, Sierra quickly ran through the money and needed more. She was all for cutting back, tightening belts, and not asking for more, but the decision went against her and more money came in, increasing the venture capitalists' stake.

At this same time, the video cartridge game market began to emerge. Companies like Activision and I-magine suddenly appeared on the market and were growing as fast as Sierra. Mattel, Texas Instruments, and Calico also joined the fray. Sierra's venture-capitalist-backed board wanted to enter the picture, too, but Roberta was wary, feeling it was better to stick with what had made them successful. Part of the reason, however, that they had joined with these guys was that they were supposedly smart, market-savvy business people.

In addition to the new product line, their partners wanted them to hire some high-powered executives. They wanted the Williamses to hire a CEO, a vice president of marketing, a vice president of sales, and a vice president of development. On the surface this sounded like sound advice, but Roberta had her doubts. Because she still didn't feel comfortable in expressing those doubts, based solely on her intuition, they went unheeded.

Roberta and Ken agreed that if they were to hire these people they had to come on-board with the same vision as them. They had to follow their lead. The company had grown to about 120 employees when the shift toward video cartridge games took place. Sierra began producing cartridges for every machine on the market. In the meantime, the computer game business was barely surviving the lack of attention. The executives that had been hired were focused completely on the video cartridge business.

The ultimate saving grace for Sierra was IBM. They came to Sierra with a contract to create a game for the new IBM PC Junior. They wanted Roberta to design a game to utilize all the capabilities of the new machine and incorporate animation. Ken worked out a stellar deal with IBM that allowed Sierra to keep the rights to the game for all other machines. Roberta went to work with a small team of people. The hired executives weren't interested. Video games were the answer.

The Williamses went away for a vacation. Upon their return they discovered that the recently hired COO had completely restructured the company. He was no longer reporting to the Williamses. Roberta could see the fiasco coming, but was in no position to stop it. The marketplace took care of it for them. The video cartridge business went bust. Atari was, literally, shipping truckloads of cartridges into the desert and burying them beneath the sand. The market had been glutted with dozens of machines, hundreds of games, and extremely poor quality control. People quit buying the machines. Sierra's employment rolls dropped from 120 to 39. The three venture capitalists on the board were ready to sell the company. According to them, the Williamses were failures. Roberta saw it differently. "We were fine until they came along. That's the way I looked at it, because I hadn't agreed with anything that had gone on since they came into our lives." Fortunately, they still had the rights deal with IBM for what was called King's Quest.

With the video game dive, Sierra's new executives deserted ship. In order to rebuild, Sierra needed more money. The venture capitalists said no way. Every time they had tried to sell the company the Williamses blocked the sale. Then came the showdown. The venture capitalists set up a meeting with Spinnaker Software. It was their pet company run by marketing people the venture capitalists had implanted. Sierra had been constantly compared to this company that Roberta never thought much of. The venture capitalists wanted Spinnaker to come to the next board meeting, which was to be held in San Francisco, to discuss a merger/takeover.

"We knew what they were going to try and do," Roberta said as her voice took on a slightly mischievous air. "We knew we would walk into the board meeting and the two guys from Spinnaker would be there. They thought we were totally out of money and had no choice. The talk would be about integrating our company in with Spinnaker, and we'd be out of the picture, and they wouldn't have to worry about us. But I had a plan.

"I wasn't going to pander to them anymore. I wasn't going to be the quiet little girl. We weren't going to put up with this. We were going to fight for our company. And we were going to save it."

On the flight to San Francisco, Roberta outlined the plan to her husband. She told him that since they still owned the majority of the company, it couldn't be sold without them. Their mistake had been to listen to these people rather than realizing they had always been in control. She recognized that they were out of money, but King's Quest was getting excellent reviews and starting to sell. Intuitively, she knew its potential was even greater— much greater than previously expected.

"I told him, let's forget the cartridge business and go back to what we know—to adventure computer games—to what we're good at. We'll mortgage the house, and fund the company, and we'll show them who's boss."

As Roberta recounts it, the plan went like this: "The meeting began at 9:00 A.M., but instead of coming in there in our dress-up clothes like meek little children, we were going to dress in jeans. Ken would show up thirty minutes late, and I would stroll in an hour and a half after that. Ken would listen, figure out their game, and then I would come in and totally break things up. I wanted to make a statement to these people that we weren't listening to them any more. We were going back to who we were."

When Ken arrived, the Spinnaker people had been meeting with the venture capitalists for half an hour discussing what they were planning to do. He sat down and was duly filled in. An hour and a half later, Roberta strolled into the large corporate meeting room with the equally long conference table, now circled by the various males in conference. She looked at her watch and in a loud voice said, "Gosh it's late. I can't believe I overslept. I'm really sorry. So, where's the coffee?" The conferees stared at her with mouths open. "So, what're y'all talking about?" she asked, playing her part and enjoying every moment.

They started telling her all the details about how they were going to be running the business when she said, "No you're not." And then she pointed to the Spinnaker people and said, "Nobody in this entire industry takes these two guys seriously but you. And there is no way that we're going to do anything with them. So you can discuss it all you want, but I have better things to do." Ken got up with her and the two of them went to lunch.

The venture capitalists immediately bugged out. The Williamses took out a mortgage on their house, made the payroll with the money, and King's Quest started to sell. "What did we learn?" Roberta asks, knowing the answer. "Basically, to trust ourselves. That we do know more than we think we know. That we don't have to be shy, and we can take control and do this. Ever since the company has grown up and up."

As with John Sculley, this approach to business requires a decision maker to avoid Arthur C. Clarke's "failure of nerve" and "failure of imagination." The Williamses survived theirs: The failure of imagination—exhibited by the venture capitalists regarding video cartridges, and sheepishly followed by them—nearly brought the mountain of success Sierra On-Line had carefully built up crumbling to the desert floor. If Roberta Williams had not avoided a failure of nerve when she finally confronted her adversaries, she might be back at her kitchen table.

Once someone learns this lesson, it can't be lost. It's been said that "experience is not what happens to you, but what you make of what happens to you." Roberta has never gone back to being that shy girl who wouldn't stand up for what she believed. "I tend to make decisions fast, and I am a great believer in my gut feel. If it doesn't feel right to me inside, and if doesn't feel right almost immediately, I don't think we should do it."

This is an excellent way to judge decisions—if it doesn't look like you should have done it years ago, it may not be the right solution. The important step to take at this point in the process is to return to basics. For Williams, that means that the people involved "have to feel right, act right, talk right, and look right. It's a combination of factors that all have to come together and feel logical to me."

One of the difficult problems that women decision makers run into when they trust their intuition is that the men they work with don't. Another might be that men have traditionally repressed women's thinking capabilities, coveting it as their own private domain. It is a condition that women are still battling against. From a psychological perspective, this is often related to a man's undeveloped vision of a woman as a little girl. No matter how mature the woman is, the man's infantilization of the woman in his mind makes him incapable of seeing her conduct complex thinking or make real decisions.

Women have been left with little recourse. Their thinking denied, women have been forced to listen to another source for their knowledge and reasoning. This intuitive source, because of its inner processing mode, had long been cloaked in the mystic mantle of seers, fortune tellers, charlatans, and anything but reason. Male rationality scoffed. This attitude, as archaic as it may sound, still exists to a large degree today. It hovers like a dark cloud over both men and women decision makers.

Dr. Ashley Montagu, the noted anthropologist and social biologist, believes that there is another reason why women use intuition more easily. He thinks it has to do with the physical differences between the sexes. "The female's inability to cope with the physically stronger male," he said in *The Natural Superiority of Women*, "obliges her, from an early age, to develop traits that will enable her to secure her ends by other means. . . . From the earliest years, girls find it necessary to pay attention to nuances and small signs of which the male rarely recognizes the existence. Such small signs and signals tell the girl what she wants to know, and she is usually ready with her plan of action before the male has begun to react."

Judith Hall, an Assistant Professor of Psychology at Johns Hopkins University in Baltimore, reports that women are more sensitive to nonverbal communication (right brain), which of course includes the emotions, and "that they tend to be more attentive to visual cues such as facial expressions, body gestures, tone of voice, and the way people look at each other."

It should be pointed out that merely being in touch with these nuances of body language and visual cues is not necessarily all the information on which intuition relies. It is only one of the aspects. Intuition functions on a total picture of things taking place both on the exterior and interior. Attention to these physical concerns can give one a better understanding of people and can feed the intuitive process in a manner that fills in gaps in the picture.

Nonetheless, these qualities in women do foster a more receptive climate for intuition, which is a main reason why women tend to score a little better on intuitive tests than men. It's also a combination of many factors; a woman's willingness to remember nonverbal clues, her ease in tapping into her deeper emotions and acknowledging this process (receptivity), and her cultural repression by men when expressing her thoughts. This has forced women to rely more heavily on their intuition (practice). All these factors have contributed in some way to the edge women seem to have in intuitive capabilities.

In spite of these advantages, the difference between men and women on intuitive test scores is relatively small. Dr. Hall believes the findings show that by eliminating strong gender roles, these scores would come together. And men are openly listening more and more to their own intuitive voices.

Sometimes old ways die hard. As Sierra was rebounding from its video cartridge fiasco and its executive flight, Ken Williams realized he needed some more help managing the company. The company had grown back to fifty employees and Williams hired a fellow who shall remain nameless for specific legal reasons. He was hired to assist and support Ken. The first time Roberta met him, she recalls that the experience was electrifying. "I shook his hand and he looked at me and said 'Hi.' And I said to myself, 'I don't like him. I don't trust him. There's something about him.'"

She immediately told her husband, who not having learned his lesson, asked, "How can you tell anything just by shaking his hand?"

As Sierra's business continued to rebound, the board became more interested in the business. This new employee quickly began making friends with the board. He began assuming responsibilities that were Ken's and not listening to things he was asked to do. Roberta wouldn't let her feelings lie. It took her almost two years, but Ken and the board finally listened and fired the employee when they discovered that Roberta's intuitive assessment had been absolutely right. This fellow had been slowly and consciously attracting Sierra's people, their vendors, their board members, and their business, with designs of starting his own company at the expense of Sierra. Roberta had sussed it from the beginning.

Like Williams, Dr. Phillip Fine at the SPAIN Rehabilitation Hospital in Birmingham, Alabama, knew better too. He was responsible for hiring a rehabilitation scientist for the hospital. SPAIN is one of the leading spinal chord injury hospitals in the country. Fine had been given the "opportunity" to interview a young rehab scientist whose family name was very well-known in the rehabilitation field. Dr. Fine had received a recommendation from the Paralyzed Veterans Association about this young lady, who was already at the doctoral level. He brought her to town and they met in his office. "Intuitively," he said, "based on all the people I'd hired and fired over the years, a red light started flashing. Something was not right. I was extremely uncomfortable.

"We went through the typical drill of going out to dinner with a couple of colleagues and our wives," Dr. Fine recalled. "We were at a particularly difficult time. We needed some help, and this person had a well-known name. Everybody said okay. We invited the woman to make a presentation to our faculty in a setting that we call 'grand rounds.' It didn't go well. And this was nagging at me. I just didn't feel right with this. But everyone told me to hire her. Hire her. So, I hired her. It was a disaster. And it wasn't that it was a self-fulfilling prophesy. I didn't set her up for failure. It was horrible."

Within four months this lady had alienated virtually everyone in Dr. Fine's department. She was bitter. She was cynical. She walked around with a chip on her shoulder. "Intellectually," Fine said, "she was a brilliant woman. But I didn't listen to that intuitive sense that told me this person was not appropriate for this group. I didn't follow my gut instinct. It destroyed my office and it destroyed a relationship with a colleague who began seeing her socially. I found out that she was a woman who would verbally attack anyone, including the person who happened not to be in the room." This included Fine.

Given that information, Dr. Fine knew what he had to do. "Quoting Machiavelli, 'Let all the blood flow in the street at once.' That's what I did. I walked into her office and said, 'This is what you said, and this is what you did.' Her mouth fell open, and she said, 'I didn't mean it like that.' and I said, 'It doesn't matter, you're finished. Go.' That was not even a calculated risk on my part. Here was a female. We're talking equal employment opportunity; we're talking heavy stuff. But I knew in my mind I'd given her the benefit of the doubt to the point where I even went back to her professor at Rutgers and asked, 'What is wrong with this woman?' When I sensed his equivocation, I made my decision instantly. This was a cancer in the operation.

"I told my secretary, 'I didn't follow my instincts and we paid for this one. Every time I've followed my intuition I've been right." Dr. Fine sees his intuition as a survival mechanism telling him "which door to open, and how many shells are in the chamber." When he didn't listen to it, he nearly blew his head off with a bullet he saw—but decided to ignore.

Often, without being aware of these intangibles, a decision maker's only recourse is to simply trust what they know and be receptive to what comes. Williams likens the process to her writing. "One thing I've learned as a writer," she says, "is I can't sit with my head in my hands, asking what should I do? What does this character do? What's the story? I have an idea in my head, and I mull it over when I'm doing the laundry, driving the car, or listening to the radio. Then it comes and I write it down. Decisions are the same for me."

Fortunately for Roberta, her partner/husband is now listening and trusting Roberta's ability. The business has continued to grow and they have begun acquiring other businesses, including a merger with the Prodigy database. Ken now insists that she be a part of every interview and decision. "We go over each and every résumé, talk about what personality traits we want in our executives, who would best fit in with the future of the company. He's trusting my intuition. And we've hired the people I've felt strongly about, and there's a very good working relationship."

From the battlements of King's Quest I through the 3-D wonders of King's Quest VI, the Williamses have fought their way back and rebuilt their company from ground zero to a $57 million business with 560 employees. Sierra On-line has survived the fray by remaining connected to what they knew. They never succumbed to their own failure of nerve, but thrived on the success of their remarkable imaginations.

3

JOHN ROLLWAGEN

THE FASTEST ANSWERS IN THE WORLD

The team that became great didn't start off great—it learned how to produce extraordinary results.

PETER M. SENGE

LEADERS ARE NOT chosen, they emerge. They step forward and assume the responsibility, the accountability. They realize, much like Ira Glasser says, that "if the things you cared about were going to be done, you were going to have to do them." John Rollwagen, chairman and CEO of Cray Research, Inc., always knew he would emerge. He just wasn't sure where.

One summer while an undergraduate electrical engineering student at the Massachusetts Institute of Technology, Rollwagen needed a job. He turned to a man that been very influential in his life for many years, his former scout master, George Hanson. Hanson was working for Control Data Corporation when he hired his young protégé. It was here that Rollwagen first heard the name of this intriguing fellow named Seymour Cray.

A few years later, as commencement exercises were underway at Harvard's Business School, Rollwagen pondered his future. As he reached out and received his master's degree he recalls that he thought, "This is neat, but now I'd like to get in business with somebody maybe one-tenth as good as Seymour Cray. He could do the technical stuff and I could do the business stuff, and we'd have a great little company." Eleven years later, Rollwagen's vision actually happened.

Cray Research builds the biggest, fastest, and most powerful supercomputers in the world. By all accounts, it should have never been able to build one computer, let alone the twenty years' worth it has produced. Cray is currently working on its fifth generation of supercomputers, and, even though they're up against the likes of IBM, Fujitsu, and NEC, they still build the best. Cray's Vice-President of Corporate Communications, Frank Parisi, calls it a "goofy little company." But this goofy little company is worth $1 billion and employs 5,500 people. Its founder, Seymour Cray, has moved on to pursue new challenges and Rollwagen stepped in to lead the company.

Rollwagen's office at Cray is small and the lights tend to be low. He has a dark hard-wood, stand-up desk at which he does most of his work. There are a couple of pictures on the wall: one of his wife and children; the other, a picture of Elvis on the moon. There is also a framed copy of two front page pictures from the local newspaper. Both show Rollwagen conducting tours of the computer center, one with Dan Quayle and one with Al Gore. During the 1992 campaign both of these gentlemen came to Cray to talk about high technology. For Quayle's visit, they showed him a simulation of a new golf club with a bigger sweet spot—very golfer friendly. Quayle was very interested. In contrast, Gore requested seeing the global environmental models Cray had developed, and while one of Cray's experts was demonstrating it, Gore took the mouse and began manipulating it to get information about environmental pollution in Tennessee.

Rollwagen's personal environment is very understated. Unlike the throne rooms of some CEOs, this a working office. The rest of the surroundings at Cray also reflect Rollwagen's sense of the world. The walls are filled with art, produced mostly by local artists. Rollwagen, himself an accomplished photographer, shows his work as well. It's his belief that creative scientists and creative artists have a lot in common. Each are trying in their own way to push the limits of what they know.

As Rollwagen says, "This is the kind of place where we don't have a lot of rules. In fact, we have a harder time getting people to leave at night than we do having to tell them what time to come in in the morning."

The environment at Cray is at the heart of its success. Rollwagen has learned the secrets from the master, Seymour Cray. Rollwagen has watched Cray carefully, "The thing that he was so good at," Rollwagen says, "without articulating it, was to put other people in the same kind of intuitive environment that he puts himself into, and it works. To some extent, we've been able to institutionalize an environment for creativity, which is very intuitive." This environment has to do with people who know each other well, and who work in small groups. The communication in these groups is very straightforward and often not complete. "You understand each other," Rollwagen explains, "and you know what's happening." It's an environment where the deadlines are clear and there are never enough resources to really get the job done. This means all the data, equipment, and tools that are needed can't be acquired. It also means that there are no back up plans. "Under these conditions," Rollwagen says, "people begin to operate at an intuitive, creative level, because they have no alternatives. They don't have the time to do the rational thing. They don't have the data, they don't have the tools, they don't have the money, so they do it anyway. People react very similarly in that environment. They start moving at a different pace to get things done."

Since 1987 Cray Research has been under increasingly stiff competition, and getting things done at an accelerated pace has become essential. For twenty years Cray Research was the dominant force in supercomputers. But, according to Rollwagen, that dominance has handicapped them. "We have a history, a constituency of customers that have very high expectations," Rollwagen says. "While they want us to be pioneers, they don't want us to change anything. We have a lot of people in the company who feel the same way."

One area of change that has consumed a great deal of time and energy for Rollwagen has been the appearance of massively parallel processing (MPP). Massively parallel processors gang together thousands of inexpensive microprocessors and then use software to break down scientific and engineering challenges into byte-size bits. Many computer theorists believe this approach holds the keys to unleashing the "teraflop," a trillion mathematical operations a second. In the supercomputer world, the only thing that counts is ever increasing speed and volume. Why is this incomprehensible speed necessary? According to an interview in Forbes magazine, Rollwagen believes, "A scientist that knows how to use a supercomputer effectively can make progress ten times faster than a scientist that can't. That says that a country that does not have supercomputers is going to fall behind."

For example, one medical application of the supercomputers is the decoding of the human genome. The worldwide race to accomplish this genetic mapping could lead to pharmaceutical developments worth hundreds of billions of dollars for the country that wins. Massively parallel processors can increase processing speed and reduce cost. Cray Research's biggest and most powerful machines cost close to $30 million each. Massively parallel processors cost between $1 and $4 million.

Rollwagen feels Cray has successfully met the challenge of its MPP competitors, but to do so required some high level intuitive decision making, bordering on what Rollwagen feels was almost outright spontaneity. In the late seventies, Rollwagen and Seymour Cray had gone off to England with their first supercomputer, hailed then as the world's most powerful computer. While there, ICL in the UK introduced a product called DAP—the distributor array processor—which was the first massively parallel processor ever built. Everyone descended upon Cray and Rollwagen peppering them with questions like, "Isn't this development going to put you guys out of business? And, good as the Cray is, isn't this a better way of doing things?" Cray replied that parallelization was an interesting concept that would be part of the future. He noted,"There's some difficult software challenges and hardware issues. And I think I want to pursue that. The smallest matrix I can think of is two by two, so I'm going to build a four-processor machine." Which he eventually did. He called it the Cray 2. It was, again, the fastest computer in the world.

Rollwagen's response was that "It's obviously promising for the future," noting the lower price as well. Rollwagen, ever the businessman, continued, "So when it comes time to make a twenty million dollar version, Cray will do it."

Jump forward in time to 1990. Cray Research has initiated a massively parallel processing project, but it is still very much in its early development. "In typical fashion," Rollwagen explains, "we were setting a target for a maximum machine to be delivered in 1994." But then something happened. Rollwagen was addressing a group called FCCST (pronounced "fixit") a federal government interagency committee that tries to look at high-performance computing. He had just been asked about Cray's efforts in this realm. "And I made a decision in the presence of my colleagues," he says, "but without talking about it a lot with my people, I announced that we would have an initial version of the machine available in 1992. It was spontaneous, because at the point it was clear we might have the best machine in 1994, but that would be too late. We had talked about an interim vehicle, a scaled down version of the '94 machine, that could possibly be built, and it seemed appropriate to me to just say it and do it. So, I put us on record, and we're doing it."

Rollwagen admits he doesn't take such unexpected steps often. "I do try and listen to my bones," he says. "The decisions I make are fairly fundamental and strategic. And I try to be particularly sensitive to the people around—not just what do they wish would happen, but what are they really thinking, because they know more than I do." Rollwagen believes part of his job is to help his people form an opinion about a decision and then integrate their thinking into his. "I'm a pretty good synthesizer," he says. "I can take a series of opinions and without articulating it at the moment, a decision becomes clear. Then I articulate it."

Making decisions utilizing others' input demands flexibility. It means a decision maker must be willing to change his or her mind. Rollwagen believes he's always willing to change his mind. In computer circles, changes are a matter of course and are usually characterized as further development. But then he learned his craft from a master developer, Seymour Cray.

In the early days of Cray Research, Rollwagen would take people out to meet Cray. People were always thrilled to meet him because he was quite famous and rather reclusive. They would talk about computers for a while and then the conversation would become more general. By nature, Cray is a very thoughtful man. One question people were fond of asking him was his opinion on the future of the world over the next four or five years. He would carefully lay out his opinions. "The story he would come up with," Rollwagen recalls, "was eternally consistent with everything that had happened to date. You'd leave the meeting thinking, my God, I understand now what the world is going to be like in five years' time. I don't even have to think about it anymore. That's obviously the answer."

As people started to come to visit Cray more often, occasionally groups would come on successive days. Rollwagen reports that the same thing would happen. Cray would describe the future and it would take into account everything that had gone on up to that point, differing just enough to encompass the previous day's events. "He always had a plan and a strategic vision, and he changed it every day." Rollwagen paused a second to reflect and then said, "You need to do both."

Running a highly competitive billion-dollar company requires of its leaders an impeccable sense of time, clear objectives, and an ability to deliver, even when delivery means completely changing everything that's gone before. In 1981, just nine years after its founding, Cray Research had accomplished all of its original goals. With more than one thousand employees and assets over $100 million, Seymour Cray was restless. He had made his life taking radical ideas from their inception and making them fabulously successful. In 1957 Cray presented Univac, his employer, with an ambitious project. When he was refused funding, he left to join William Norris and his fledgling Control Data Corporation. In 1972, CDC wasn't ready to take the leap Cray wanted to take. He left to pursue his own vision of supercomputing, which revolutionized the world's vision of the power of computers.

Now, having gone from zero to ten with his projects, Cray found himself once again staring at a ten. Rollwagen came to his friend and mentor, recognizing Seymour's symptoms. "This isn't working anymore, is it?" Cray agreed. Rollwagen then suggested they find a way to make it work. Cray agreed again. They worked out an arrangement for Cray to become an independent contractor. This meant he wouldn't be involved in the running of the company but would still work for it, benefiting from its resources but having the freedom to go back to zero. Rollwagen's vision was to take the company from ten to one hundred.

Eight years later, on the phenomenal success of Cray Research's advancements, Rollwagen had brought the company to one hundred. These innovations included things like gold on gold bonding for faster electronic transmissions and figuring out how to make electricity run in only one direction rather than its slower and less efficient back and forth path. In the meantime, Seymour Cray had brought his Cray 3 technology from a zero to an eight. He was having some trouble with one aspect of the computer, a new technology using gallium-arsenide chips. He was looking to go back to zero, and Rollwagen had his sights set on 1,000.

Evidence of Cray's eagerness to start over came when he moved from his long-time hometown of Chippewa Falls, Wisconsin, to Colorado Springs, Colorado. Chippewa Falls, a short drive from Cray Research's Eagen, Minnesota, headquarters near Minneapolis, was the place all of Cray's computers had been built. To Rollwagen's perception, this was Seymour's attempt to get as far away from Cray Research as he could to restart the Cray 3. Rollwagen gave his blessing.

The folks working in Chippewa Falls were shocked. Twenty-five hundred people worked there. Many of them had never met Seymour Cray, yet felt intimately involved with him, and couldn't understand how he could leave. Once they got over the shock of Cray's departure, they were disappointed and angry. This guy had brought them out to the wilderness to build his computers and now he was splitting? Finally, the troops accepted Cray's departure. They turned their attention back to building their computers. The machine they were all currently involved with, the C-90, could be tweaked, twisted, and sped up to be faster than the Cray 3 and still get to market before it. The race was on.

About six months later, after a great deal of mulling and reflection, Rollwagen realized he had created an untenable situation. There was Seymour in Colorado, whose Cray 3 had been delayed temporarily by the move, and the C-90, utilizing more evolutionary technology than the Cray 3 and proceeding rapidly under a young, highly motivated design team in Chippewa Falls. Both products were squarely aimed at the same market and destined to arrive at the same time. They utilized different technology, but both were extremely competitive. "It was like having a set of twins in utero, but they had different blood types," Rollwagen explained. "They couldn't coexist in the same womb. Something had to be done. And it was Solomon's choice." Then, while Rollwagen was heading toward a major corporate and strategic decision, the recession tipped everything groundward.

Everyone was starting to feel the financial pinch. Cray had invested about $50 million into the development of the Cray 3 and an equal amount into the C-90. Rollwagen knew something had to be done, but what? "We couldn't stop Seymour's project," he said, "I mean, come on, his name is on the door. Besides, it was an excellent project, and there was no reason to kill it." Rollwagen's other choice was killing the C-90. But then he realized if he did that he was sending the message that there is no Cray Research without Seymour Cray. He knew that would discourage the young designers who were moving the company forward. Throughout the organization, the anxiety level was intense. Then the decision hit Rollwagen.

His recollection of that moment, crowning six months of tension and pondering, was an immediate relief—an "aha" feeling of landing on the right choice. "It was scary until it arrived," he admitted. But he knew what steps had to be taken.

Rollwagen got on a plane and flew to Colorado. Cray and Rollwagen sat down together like they had on so many occasions during their fifteen-year friendship and association. But this one was different. The level of tension was high. The conversation briefly touched on personal things, then settled down to the situation at hand. Rollwagen looked across at his friend and mentor, took a breath, and said, "Seymour, we need to split the company."

Seymour said simply, "I agree with you."

"How much money do you need to finish your project?"

"Probably one hundred million dollars."

"Fine."

The deal was made. Cray would take his Colorado Springs facility, the equipment there, and the people that were with him. These assets totaled $50 million. In addition, over the next two years, Cray would receive an additional $100 million. Cray Research would take what was left.

Rollwagen's initial perception of the situation was that he was going to go to Colorado and join Cray. "But then I realized," he says, "that decision was inappropriate for me. I'd already done that. What I hadn't done is Cray Research. It was a very personal decision. There was a lot of anxiety to begin with, but one of the things that Seymour and I were able to do as partners was be quiet and listen together." The split was very clear to Rollwagen. "It may have even been more clear to me than him," he says.

As part of the agreement, Cray Research would still own ten percent of Seymour's new company, Cray Computer Corporation.

The other ninety percent of the stock would be distributed, tax free, to Cray Research's shareholders.

A month later, when they announced their decision at Cray Research's annual meeting, the financial community didn't know what to make of this unexpected turn of events. A month earlier, Control Data Corporation had announced it was folding its supercomputer company, ETA Systems, because it was losing money.

Rollwagen's decision wasn't precipitated by ETA's collapse, though it did play a factor. On numerous occasions, Rollwagen had expressed his concerns about his big three Japanese competitors, NEC, Fujitsu, and Hitachi, trying to fill the void in American supercomputing. Supercomputers are considered vital for weapon and airline development, and there was even some speculation that Rollwagen and Cray had predicated their decision on their government contracts. The Pentagon and other government agencies require two bidders on any contract, and with the loss of ETA, there was now only one U.S. company capable of filling the bill. Rollwagen maintains that he never consulted with Washington before reaching the decision.

In a *New York Times* article David Wu, a financial analyst who is a close follower of the computer industry, thought, "It was a brilliant decision. It's a case," Wu said, "of the parts being worth more than the whole. From the country's standpoint, it's the best thing that could happen."

Gary Smaby, an analyst at Needham & Company in Minneapolis, saw more than just the benefit to the various parties and to the country. "What strikes me is the unique nature of this resolution," he said. "There has never been a deal done like it."

Immediately following the announcement, there was talk in Washington of adopting a national policy that would help American supercomputer companies. The Japanese had embraced a national doctrine nearly ten years earlier, which allowed them to drop their prices 80 percent off their list to win a contract.

Rollwagen felt the bite of foreign competition, as Cray Research's profits dropped from a 50 percent annual increase to only 10 percent. Nonetheless, he still believed they had a two-year head start on the Japanese, and the speed of their machines proved it. The Cray performance speed was over 2 billion calculations a second, compared to NEC's less than 1 billion. But staying in front isn't simply a matter of running faster. As Lewis Carroll's Alice said, "It takes all the running you can do to stay in the same place." It's also a matter of running better.

Some analysts saw the Cray/Rollwagen split as evidence that Cray Research's management was finally realizing that it was neither a small Apple-like garage computer operation nor a seat-of-the-pants organization. Rollwagen insisted, however, that Cray Research would remain as innovative and creative as ever.

One of Rollwagen's primary tools in operating his billion-dollar business is the process of visualization. At the end of every year, Rollwagen allows himself the space to literally look back on the year that has passed and to look forward. "Looking back seems so clear and logical," he says. "I can see the path quite clearly and see why things happened. I can see how to get from the present to the past. Yet, I know, if I was sitting in the past trying to visualize today, I certainly wouldn't be able to follow that path. What I can do is project myself into the future that I might like, and find my path back to where I am right now. Then that's the path I will start on. It might change, but that's what gives me the clue. If I started here and said then this will happen, followed by that, I get totally confused. I absolutely believe in visualization."

Part of Rollwagen's management process is also to meditate. "That's when my voice is very quiet," he explains. "I don't meditate to make a decision. It isn't purposeful in that sense. But it is a way of quieting down and touching earth. I don't expect to wake up from a meditation and say, 'Oh, now I understand.' I just expect to be quiet, and then I have the confidence that in some not too distant time it will find its way."

It is at the point of this quiet place when intuition is often the loudest. It is that quality that Rollwagen surmises is absolutely necessary as a leader for his organization. "Cray couldn't tolerate a leader," Rollwagen believes, "that would say, 'Okay, you're going to do this and you're going to do that, and I'm going to check on you tomorrow.'" To a certain degree, it was that position that cost Cray Research's President Marcelo Gumuclo his job.

About a year after Cray Research's split with Seymour Cray, Gumuclo made an announcement that he was resigning from Cray Research. He and Rollwagen agreed that their contrasting management styles had made it impossible to work together. As characterized in the newspapers, Gumuclo was an aggressive marketer while Rollwagen had a more wide-open management style. As Gary Smaby explained it, "Rollwagen was clearly the more visionary, long-term thinker."

The difference in management styles was quite distinct. In contrast to the more old school approach, Rollwagen says, "I may want certain things to happen, but it's more effective if I can plant seeds, and the best seeds are planted on an almost intuitive basis." It's a policy of engaging people in the problem by asking them for a solution, not telling them the solution. I find that's more easily done in a less directed, more intuitive way," Rollwagen explains.

The approach seems to be working. After the departure of Seymour Cray and Gumuclo, Rollwagen fashioned a radically different company. The product line included computers ranging in price from a $300,000 mini-supercomputer to their $30 million current version of the world's fastest computer. They also employed more than 450 software designers that would link their supercomputers with work stations, and eventually to their new line of massively parallel machines.

As a high-tech marketing specialist, Regis McKenna explains, "A decision is process. People are successful in today's world by constantly altering and adjusting to the environment. It's a constant process of change. You can't make decisions that are absolute, because there is no absolute. There are only relative situations."

Like McKenna, Rollwagen knows his process. He knows how he operates. "When I get in trouble," he says, "is when I make a list of pros and cons and go about decision making in a very rational process. I get myself confused. I can do all kinds of fancy things with spread sheets, and I love system analysis and complicated feedback systems, which comes from my engineering background. It's always fun, but it never gives me the right answer. It always comes out with something that was perfectly logical. And I look at it, and say, 'That's goofy. That isn't right.'" What gives Rollwagen the answer is to just sit quietly and let the information sink in. He doesn't like to rush a decision. "Let it come," he says. "And it does finally appear."

Rollwagen knows the value of an emotional management attitude. It's something he encourages and reinforces by his actions continually at Cray. "People see me either making decisions or acting in ways that are clearly nonrational," he says, "and it gives them permission to do it too."

Rollwagen is definitely not a traditionalist, but then his billion-dollar company was founded on its innovative combination of creativity and science. It's that willingness to listen to the creative, and to tap into the intuitive that has driven the success of Cray Research from its inception. The path may not always be clear, but the approach is. "I believe very strongly," Rollwagen says, "that many times there is no right decision but to get on with it. I don't care what you do. The important thing is to move ahead. Let's just do it, because you're not going to be right or wrong. It's just one route and you can fix it after you start. But if you never start, you never get there. That's for damn sure."

For Rollwagen, making the decision is nothing more than flipping a coin. "It's a wonderful way to make decisions," he says, "not because you do what the coin says. But because you have that instantaneous recognition when the coin hits whether you like the results or not. And that's the answer. Don't go with the coin, go with how you felt after the coin landed."

Some decisions, Rollwagen has discovered, no matter how well considered, don't work out as planned. In late December 1992, after making the drive to the family cabin for the holiday break, he received a message from Washington. President Clinton wanted Rollwagen to take a job in his administration. At the time, they had several positions in mind, but all they wanted to know at this point was if he'd be interested in coming to Washington. He told them he'd call back the next day with his answer.

Rollwagen discussed the call with his wife, Beverly. He had been at Cray Research for seventeen years. Washington would certainly provide a much different atmosphere. Within two hours, they'd made their decision. Rollwagen called Washington the same night. A month later, the job of deputy secretary of commerce was his. Taking the position meant resigning from Cray Research, but it also meant an opportunity to lead the government's policy to promote high technology.

His first experience as deputy secretary designate was meeting with the president, vice president, their wives, and all the cabinet appointees at Camp David for a weekend team-building retreat. Rollwagen was very impressed with the president and his cabinet. He left Camp David enthused and ready for work.

Unfortunately, reporting to his office on Monday changed everything. Working in Washington was very different from Cray. After three days of struggles and D.C. bureaucracy, Rollwagen's intuition told him he had made a major mistake. The starry-eyed optimism that he had arrived with had quickly dissolved into shocked realism. He went to his boss, Secretary of Commerce Ron Brown, and told him he had to quit. Brown eventually convinced Rollwagen that he was making his decision too quickly and without enough information. Things would improve, Brown promised.

On the road to confirmation, however, questions arose regarding the Cray Computer stock Cray Research had sold in November 1991. Lawrence Livermore Lab had unexpectedly canceled a major order with Cray Computers on December 19, 1991, which caused the price of Cray Computer stock to tumble. The Securities and Exchange Commission interviewed Rollwagen, who was not personally implicated in the investigation. Rollwagen was two hours from confirmation when pressure from the investigation postponed the hearing.

Rollwagen knew he had done nothing wrong and would eventually gain confirmation. But the delay gave him an opportunity. Four months had passed since he had walked into Ron Brown's office and resigned. Little had changed. This time he would listen to his intuition.

On May 20, 1993, Rollwagen made his decision. He withdrew his nomination from consideration. Rollwagen told the *New York Times* that the investigation played only a minor role in his decision. As he explained it, "I've been in the private sector for thirty years and attempted to come into the public sector cold turkey. I knew that it was different, but I didn't realize how different."

Who wouldn't be flattered and honored when the president of the United States asks you to serve? Sometimes, allowing yourself to know exactly what you know isn't enough. Unexpected circumstances arise after a decision is made, and all a decision maker can do is to move forward. In his final Washington decision, Rollwagen knew that to spend more time in the capital would not be fruitful for him or the government. A difficult decision like this one can only come from the gut. Rollwagen knew it was the right decision. It was also one he had to make alone.

MICHAEL MONDAVI

DECANTING THE RIGHT DECISIONS

In vino veritas.

PLINY

THE EXPERIENCE OF wine is in the first taste. Everything you will ever know about this fruit of the vine is revealed in that instant. Its color, its nose, and its finish. Great winemakers invest and risk everything on that first taste. The name of Mondavi has become synonymous with great California wines. Oh, there are the others, but the image of the Mondavis are seated in that first taste of their elegant, lush, sweet oak, black cherry, earthy, velvety classic wines.

The Robert Mondavi Winery was founded in 1966. It was established following the split between brothers Robert and Peter over the operations of the family's Charles Krug Winery, which their father, Cesare, had purchased in 1943. Today the third generation of Mondavis are at the helm of the Mondavi Winery. Michael runs the business, Timothy is the winemaker, and sister Marcia has assumed the East Coast marketing. This is winery as family—a feeling that extends from the houses on the property where the family lives to the employees spending their days caring for the wine. It is a devoted family. Maintaining this family business is the job of the tall, slender, and mustachioed Michael Mondavi.

Wine is a slow growth business. Plant the vines and it takes at least five years before they will produce a bottle of wine. The winery's average cash flow is twenty-eight months—from the time the grapes are crushed, the wine aged, the bottles make it to the customer, and the money is in the bank is almost two and a half years. Making business decisions in this context means that Michael Mondavi is constantly looking forward to how his decision will benefit future generations of Mondavis.

By wine standards, 1974 was a remarkable year. It was an excellent vintage with an exceptionally high volume of grapes produced—20 percent over the norm. At the same time, interest rates in the country were going up, the dollar was weak, and the European wines were in trouble. The California wines had made giant quality and quantity gains over the past couple of years, and suddenly they were hit with a surplus. Prices dropped drastically.

When the Mondavis' 1974 crop came in, they knew it was going to make a superb wine, but they also knew it was going to be bigger than they knew what to do with. Today the Mondavis bottle 100 percent of their wine. In 1974 they sold 50 percent to tank-cars and other wineries.

Mondavi had to make a quick decision. He sold the vast majority of their tank-car crop before everyone else, for $3 a gallon. They lost three-quarters of a million dollars, but they could have lost a lot more. "Our attitude was very simple," says Mondavi stretching his long runner's body, "the first loss is the best loss."

Mondavi was then advised that since the rest of the crop was nearly twice the volume of previous vintages, they would never be able to sell it. They should dump it as bulk for $2 a gallon. Mondavi said, "No. The wine was too damn good. We'll find a way to sell it.

"The toughest part of that decision was we had our own advisers telling us from their perspective we should do 'a' when I knew from my experience that my gut was saying we should do 'b.' I didn't want to unilaterally do 'b.' So we tried to convince them that we were right, and couldn't." Mondavi knew what he had to do.

The Mondavi winery is located in Oakville, California, near the middle of the Napa Valley, a narrow sluice of fertile land that produces some of the finest wine grapes in the country. Mornings have a special quality here. It's the light, the way the sunlight breaks across Stag's Leap Mountain and filters down the valley. Out on the back narrow lanes between the vineyards there are no phones for Mondavi to answer. In the morning, he runs, and his thoughts are free to travel inside, while his physical being is engaged with the pattern of his steps. It's a time when he allows himself free thought. "You need free thought," he says, "to let [a decision] get into your head, to let it fester, and then just think about it while you're running, without a Walkman or radio. I let the thoughts flow through as the tides would flow." Then, all of a sudden, a wave crashed on the beach. "Why didn't I think about that sooner. It's so simple." The decision had made itself.

Everyone sitting at the morning breakfast table knew Michael had come to some sort of decision. Those that knew him recognized the signs. When he was gathering data about a decision, he ate very rapidly. When he was about to make a decision, he ate very slowly. Now he chewed each mouthful deliberately.

The notion that had surfaced on those back, vine-scented lanes was this: "In order to understand the best wines in the world, you had to taste the best wines in the world. It was not just a matter of saying ours is better. We had to see if we belonged on the same table. Because we'd almost gone bankrupt, and now had this huge crop of 1974 cabernet, we had to increase our sales, collect the money, pay the bank, or say good-bye."

All the superlatives had been used about the 1974 cabernet. It was the best cabernet Mondavi had ever produced, but how did they communicate that to the people they wanted to buy the wine—the top quality restaurant owner, the maitre d' who buys the wines, and the retail wine shops? "We couldn't compete with the big boys," Mondavi recalls. "We couldn't give them ten dollars off a bottle or send them on a trip to the Bahamas. We're just not that size. We didn't feel we could do it through print or the electronic media either. We also didn't have enough people to sit down and have an individual tasting with each of our customers. And we found that by tasting just one wine alone, everyone says it's a nice wine, but it's no big deal."

So, Michael put forward his idea. "Why don't we do what we do when we're tasting wines ourselves to see how they rate? But let's do it on a large scale. Let's have five hundred of the top restaurants and wine shops in California come to the winery and we'll taste the five Bordeaux first growths (the finest French wines produced) and our cabernet and cabernet reserve. We'll taste them blind."

The first reaction to Mondavi's suggestion was, "Do you know how much those first growths cost?"

"I said, 'So what?' If we do it and we come out first, that's bad, because the wine is too different. If we come out last, that's bad, because it's so different. But if we come out second through sixth, we've won." Mondavi convinced his detractors, and they gave it a try. They brought fifty of the state's top restaurateurs to the tasting at the winery and opened the concealed bottles of Chateau Lafite Rothschild, Chateau Mouton Rothschild, Chateau Latour, Chateau Margaux, Chateau Haut-Brion, and Mondavi's two cabernets. The tasters could rate the bottles and write down their ratings or just keep their ratings to themselves. When the results were tabulated by two of the restaurateurs, they announced first what the wines were. Mondavi's wines came in third and fourth—exactly where Mondavi had hoped. These people represented the finest restaurants in California. For the most part, they had never tasted a California wine next to a great first growth Bordeaux. The prejudice had always been that California made a nice wine, but if you wanted a great wine you had to have a Lafite or Haut-Brion.

As Mondavi recalls, "The response to that tasting was mind-boggling. We immediately set up eight more around the state. In fourteen months we sold two years' equivalent of wines, and we were on allocation. That was really just intuition." In addition to their success, Mondavi became the largest U.S. purchaser of first growth wines, ordering hundreds of cases. The practice proved so successful, it's been continued for over a decade and a half, to the present day.

Mondavi has had his share of wine mentors. His father is considered by many to be one of the most influential winemakers in the world. Robert was a man who went palate to palate with the French and their attitude about California wines. He then brought Barone Mounton Rothschild on board to create a wine called Opus One, which today is renowned as one of the world's great wines. It is widely considered to be the first truly international wine. Mondavi learned a great deal from his father. But one of his greatest lessons came from the largest wine producer in the United States Ernest Gallo. It was a lesson Mondavi never forgot.

Mondavi had just been elevated to vice president of marketing and sales, and Gallo came up to him at a function. He pulled the young Mondavi aside and said, "I understand you're going to be getting involved with the marketing?"

Michael said proudly, "Yes, Mr. Gallo."

"Do you know what I do?" the elder statesman of wine asked.

"Well, you run Gallo Winery," Mondavi replied.

"Do you know what I do?" Gallo repeated.

"Well, you probably coordinate the long range plans and . . . " Mondavi continued outlining the various specifics, trying to show off his knowledge of the business.

Gallo said, "No. I call on my customers. I call on the retailers. I don't just go to the distributor, I don't just listen to my people. I call on the account. That way I can get a pulse and a feel of what is happening. I don't get my information through five or six filters. Once I've done that, then I talk to my people and my distributors."

Mondavi just stared at this California wine legend and Gallo dropped his voice. "You'll never be as big as Gallo. You will never be as busy. And if *I* can call on the accounts and get the direct input and the pulse, so can *you*."

As Mondavi reflects, "I found that to be extremely valuable advice, to get a pulse on what is happening in the wine market. If you listen to the sales reps and distributors, they're about six months behind the market. If you go right to the retailer or the restaurateur, you're right there.

"For example, last week in San Francisco, four of the top restaurants had fewer than 25 percent of the seats filled. These are quality restaurants, and I check with them each week on their occupancies. As a result of these calls, I know that forty-five to sixty days from now they'll be ordering less wine from the distributor, and sixty days from then, the distributor will be ordering less wine from us. Two hundred days from now, we will be looking at charts that say our sales are slowing down, and that's too late to respond." Mondavi probably makes fifteen calls a week to various cities throughout the country and from that he gets a fairly accurate pulse on those markets. "It lets me know things are proceeding as planned," he says, "or it gives me an early warning that we better see if the promotions and activities we planned are going to be sufficient to accomplish our goals."

Even the short-term decision Mondavi makes have long-term consequences. In fact, the primary basis for all his decisions is on long-term plans. It is this perspective of the future, where decisions are not pressured by the quarterly report mentality, that separates management from leadership. Management tends to concentrate on the short term, while leadership must take in the total operational perspective, with a view as to what can and will be done in the future.

The biggest decision Mondavi and his family have had to make in support of this philosophy was buying back their business. They had been partners with Seattle's Rainier Brewing Company until Rainier was purchased by Hamms. Being part of a holding company was not what the Mondavis had in mind.

They retained a management consulting firm and asked their

accountants to help out. The Mondavis still owned 50 percent of the voting stock in the winery and they had some money to invest. They wanted to know if they should invest it in other businesses to diversify the family portfolio or buy back some of the family business. Both the consulting firm and the CPA recommended that they not invest more money in the wine business because it was too capital intensive. Their suggestions were to buy things like shopping centers and apartment houses.

The family got together to consider the recommendations. They talked about it and then decided. The decision was to back the winery. The Mondavis based the decision on four factors. First, they wanted to be a privately held company. Second, they liked the lifestyle of the wine business. Third, their estimate of the growth and the potential of the wine business exceeded the estimate of their consultants. Finally, they realized that they didn't know anything about running properties or portfolios. What they knew was managing vineyards, making wine, and marketing and selling wine for a profit. As Mondavi recalls, "By getting the others' input and going through the evaluation with them, it formulated in our minds what our abilities, our strengths, and our weaknesses were, and what we wanted to do." The Mondavis decided to stick with what they already knew.

Once they purchased the company back, they could make the next long-term decision. They looked at the overall objectives of the family, and, in spite of further calls from their advisers to diversify, they decided to purchase another winery, Vichon.

Lying in the shadow of the Transamerica Pyramid, about thirty miles south of their Napa Valley vineyard, are the Mondavis' San Francisco offices. It was here that Mondavi met with the owners of the small boutique winery, Vichon. Their wines had been generating great excitement and considerable profit.

The principals of Vichon and their attorneys met with Mondavi and his representatives. The Vichon winery fit exactly into the Mondavi picture. But there was trouble. Vichon was waffling on the deal. Their asking price was still too high, and the negotiations were getting nowhere. Michael Mondavi had had enough. He and his attorney walked out of the meeting. "We closed the books," said Mondavi. "We told them if they were interested to call us back, because we weren't calling back. And we meant it. Then, on Wednesday of the following week they called us. 'It might be interesting if we got together again.' We did, and all of a sudden we were rehashing the whole thing over again. I said, 'This can't go on. I'm interested in buying, but I'm only going to buy it if it is something that is going to work out to where we can make it a viable business. If you want to sell it for more than it's worth, don't talk to somebody in the business.'"

Then it suddenly hit Mondavi. While the opposing attorneys were debating over an issue, Mondavi wrote down a figure on a piece of paper and handed it to his attorney. There was a pause and Mondavi went over to Vichon's senior attorney and handed him the scrawled figure. "This is our final offer. If you will agree to it right now, I'm sure I can convince our board to go along with it. But I want an answer now." The offer was about $100,000 more than previously authorized.

The senior attorney said, "Done." Vichon's two owners stood up and said,"What do you mean!?" Their attorney took them outside for a quick chat and a minute later the deal was set.

Mondavi's sudden intuitive sense that this was the right amount and that this was the time to offer it was not based on marketing figures or corporate strategic goals. This was face to face negotiations, and Mondavi's decision came from his ability to synthesize all he knew about wine and people. It also came from his confidence in his intuitive voice, which had laid out the whole picture to him.

The comfort Mondavi felt with Vichon was proved over the next few years. The Vichon label worked well for Mondavi from a quality and image perspective. With seven hundred wineries in the region producing excellent wines, everyone has to ensure that their quality and image are at their highest. Vichon's reputation increased sales phenomenally throughout the west.

The next step was to bring out a less expensive Vichon wine.

Mondavi put forward Vichon Coastal Selection, a quality wine in the $10-a-bottle range as opposed to the $20-and-up range.

There were a number of people in the organization that didn't have the same comfort level as Mondavi with this idea. There were those who felt it would be confusing in the marketplace or for the distributors and sales people. There were those who thought it might downgrade the overall image of the Napa Valley and the venerated Stag's Leap district where Vichon is produced.

Mondavi looked to what Barone Philippe de Rothschild had done in the 1950s with Mouton Cadet. As Mondavi explains, "Rothschild was chastised in Bordeaux for coming out with an ordinary Bordeaux and putting the Mouton name on it. Rothschild felt he was accomplishing a number of things: One, he was giving a very good value/quality price relationship; and two, he was introducing a whole new group of people to Bordeaux wines, and in particular to Chateau Mouton Rothschild. I think that type of rationale is just as viable today for Vichon."

In this instance, Mondavi's comfort level was again right. Vichon Coastal Selection was introduced to the market and sold out within six months—a phenomenal success.

The development of Mondavi's decision-making process did not take place in a vacuum. His mentors never told him what to do, they questioned him. Why are you doing this? Did you think about these consequences? Did you consider this idea? "I think the ability to make good decisions is in your training, which comes after university or grad school. That's where the confidence comes from. In an area where I don't have confidence, I can't get that free thought, like when I'm running. And if I can't get that free thought, then I can't get comfortable with a decision."

Mondavi finds that the toughest and most nerve-wracking decisions for him are those when, very early in the process, everyone is in complete agreement. "When something is too easy, I start looking around and asking what's wrong." But one such decision was the absolutely right one. It returned Mondavi to the notion of the first loss is the best loss.

In 1990 a devastating problem struck without warning. The menace was an aphid-like bug called *Phylloxera*. It is literally a louse that hides deep in the soil and feeds on the root systems of grape vines. It is again threatening the entire $3 billion American wine industry. A little over a century ago, it almost wiped out the wine industry worldwide.

The only way to fight this bug is to replace the vines with a rootstock that will resist them. When the problem surfaced in 1990, few growers really understood the peril that Napa, Sonoma, Mendocino, and Lake counties faced. It took Mondavi ten days to go from thinking there was no problem to realizing it was a devastating occurrence. He made a major decision. The Mondavis spent $1 million buying new rootstock less than ten days after first hearing of the bug's arrival. Mondavi wanted to make sure that they had the supply, varieties, and quality of stock they needed to survive the next three- to four-year period. He knew full well that Mondavi would have to convert the vineyard infected by the *Phylloxera* to young, healthy vineyards to weather the storm.

"The concern was," Mondavi says, his fields now secure, "that if we weren't among the first that bought the stock, there wouldn't be enough available of the varieties we needed to do a quality job." They bought the rootstock and took ownership of it, as opposed to buying futures of stock. This was done so that none of the giant multinational companies, such as Nestlé or Heublein, that owned wineries could go in and simply buy the whole nursery, leaving other vineyards unable to obtain resistant rootstock.

"We had to make sure we could protect ourselves if they did that. Now, the multinationals might buy the ground, buildings, and business, but we owned those little plants." That little bit of rapid, gut-level, corporate decision making may have cost the Mondavis a good deal of money, but, as the rest of the wine growing region realized the extent of the problem, it saved them a considerable fortune over what it might have cost them. It might never have happened that way if they weren't already aware that often the first lost was the best loss.

This was a decision that was definitely made for the future

generation of the business. And Mondavi is quick to point out, "The future generations of the business are not just the immediate family, but the future generations of employees as well." The Mondavi organization has always realized and respected the value of its people.

"It all comes down to people," says Mondavi. "We try to operate relatively decentralized. For example, I do not tell our vice president of marketing and sales that he can or cannot do a certain kind of sales promotion." Mondavi will give him his comments, and the VP will take them into account. But he knows that if he disagrees with Mondavi and decides to go the way he planned, Mondavi won't stop him. Mondavi understands that the VP is more involved in the day to day operations and understands the detail more than Mondavi. "Because the way he has done things has worked so beautifully, I have comfort in deferring to his judgment," Mondavi says.

"We all look in the mirror and think we can make the best decision," Mondavi says confidently, "when realistically, we have a lot of people who understand the detail and have better information about those areas than I have. It's very important to delegate the decision to people who understand the philosophy and direction of the business to make the decision. And we've found time after time they make excellent decisions."

In the parlance of the Just-in-Time, Total Quality Management scheme of things, this is known as supporting the "Thinking Worker." This notion says that intelligence and creativity are equally distributed throughout an organization. They don't just lie at the top.

Integrating this methodology into the framework of an organization is not an easy task, but it is without peer in bringing employees into the company's operations. As Mondavi makes clear, "Both the exciting and frustrating part of any major decision is that there are times when you know what you want to do, but if you just unilaterally go off and do it, a lot of people won't support it and make it successful. You need to go through the education process, the discussion, and idea exchange to refine the details of the decision from the input of the people involved. You can't just unilaterally say, this is the direction we're going and we want you all to step in place."

Dr. Lew Allen, former director of NASA/Caltech's Jet Propulsion Lab, deputy director of the CIA, and former director of the National Security Agency, has had a lot of experience in this area, and he concurs with Mondavi. "It is important that I make decisions that have been constructed and developed in such a way that the organization will be able and willing to carry them out. There's a futility to decisions which are made in a private office," Dr. Allen says, "and then fall on an organization in a manner in which they are not prepared or motivated to execute them. Many of the most difficult decisions I make are just as much about making wise decisions as [they are about] making decisions which can be executed. Sometimes that means the decision is not what I personally would have thought to be the best answer, but ends up being the answer which is necessary to have the organizational system then move to implement it directly."

For Allen, this also requires pushing decision making down in the organization. He is a firm believer in "getting leadership arising from the lowest levels of the organization." He has found that it is from within these ranks of thinking workers that an organization or company should be seeking answers about the strengths and weaknesses of its decisions.

As any organizational leader understands, letting others make meaningful decisions and implementing and supporting those decisions immediately brings people into the process. A successful business is not just about what the company produces, it's also about the people that produce it. "People say we are in the wine business," Mondavi notes. "We are in the people business. And if we can get the people who are doing the job to be involved in making those day to day decisions and teach our people to be aware of the thought process, they are going to be more valuable to themselves and far more valuable to us."

Mondavi's words are not just lip service. Walk into his Oakville wine cellar and you will see hourly employees working together in teams, solving problems on a daily basis. You will see training sessions introducing the workers to the latest ideas on how to run their operations more effectively. And you will see incentive programs honoring their accomplishments. These are not organizational decisions that are spelled out in a scripted business analysis. These are company-wide decisions to do business by listening and following the input of people and trusting in what they know. As Mondavi says, "It's the absolute smartest thing we can do for the long-term health of the business."

MARGARET LOESCH

THE RIGHT TOON AT THE RIGHT TIME

I do not believe. . . . I know.

C. G. JUNG

IN THE WORLD of blue Smurfs, green turtles, Tiny Toons, and Baby Muppets, there is simply no one who compares with Margaret Loesch. At forty-five, Loesch (pronounced Lesh) is known as "the Queen of Cartoon." She is also known as the president of the Fox Children's Network—the only woman president of a major television network in the United States. She sits behind that gray-toned desk because she's the best. And she's the best because when tough creative decisions have to be made, she consistently out zaps and kablows the competition time and again. How? "I listen," she says.

Having been responsible for the development and production of more than one hundred children's television series and specials, Loesch's ability to listen and tune into the pulse of her audience is truly remarkable. "I try to get as much information as possible about an issue. I seek advice from people I respect. Sometimes it's a chore, because I want to jump in, but I will make myself listen. Then I absorb the information, and, being sensitive to everything around me, something clicks, and I decide what to do."

That click doesn't arise from the ether. It comes from Loesch's knowledge of her field, her options, the people she's working with, and the repercussions that might arise. "Little decisions are easy. They're spontaneous. But important things get clouded, because they are so important. Ultimately, I do what I think is best. I literally say to myself, 'Now what do you really think, Margaret? What do you really feel? You've heard all this. Are you feeling this way because the president of the company or the staff thinks this way or that?' I just have to listen for that gut. Every mistake I have ever made in this business was because I didn't follow my own instinct."

When it comes to making that tough decision she believes, "You have to not be afraid. Well, you can be afraid, but you have to be willing to take a chance."

Loesch's career in Hollywood began with her willingness to take a chance. She grew up in Pass Christian, Mississippi, just over the border from New Orleans, further away from Hollywood than mere distance might suggest. This small gulf town, once the home of Confederate President Jefferson Davis, is obviously a much smaller and quieter town than its neighbor, New Orleans.

Pass Christian certainly wasn't big enough for the drive Loesch felt. Out of school, she took a job as a broker for a securities company. "I thought I was good," she says, recalling the images vividly, "but I guess I wasn't very good, because when I resigned the head of personnel said to me 'Let me give you a little advice. You should be in a different business, one where you can be more creative.'"

His perception was that she'd come into the brokerage business and wanted to change things in nontraditional ways. "That scares people when you're dealing with their money," he told her. "You ought to be in a business where you can foster ideas."

Upon reflection, Loesch packed her bags and headed for California. She had no money, no job, and she discovered no one would hire her. Finally, in desperation, she returned to brokerage and got a good offer. She would be an assistant cashier, which would pay about $1,000 a month.

A couple of days before the offer had come through, a friend had suggested she look for work at the TV networks. "What do I know about TV?" she asked. Despite her lack of credentials, she checked it out. She drove to CBS in Hollywood and asked the personnel chief if they had a management training program. The man with whom she spoke said to her, "All our girls start as typists."

"I'll never forget this," Loesch says, a look of ultimate satisfaction crossing her face. "I've never been much of a feminist, but 'all of our *girls*.' He was a terrible, nasty man." Nonetheless, she was desperate, and she said she'd be willing. Then came the typing test.

Loesch's typing was fine until someone tested it. The man put her in a little room with a large institutional clock on the wall that loudly ticked off the seconds. "I'm taking this test and looking at this clock, tick, tick, tick, ticking. I typed eighteen words a minute before they counted the mistakes. It was terrible. He came back and said, 'Don't call us.'"

An hour later, Loesch had an appointment at ABC. She drove her borrowed '54 Chevy across town on a rainy L.A. December afternoon. "I was feeling pretty bad, because this man made me feel like I was really a hick from Mississippi." At ABC, things were different. She met Ruth Avery. "I'll never forget her. She was so sweet to me. I told her the story of my experience with CBS. She was so outraged on my behalf that she said, 'Well, let's just say you typed 40 words a minute.' And she wrote it on the form. I was aghast. I thought, oh my God, they're going to catch me."

Avery told Margaret, "You know, I think you have some real potential. And I think that if you would be willing to start as a clerk, there could be opportunities for you." Once again, eager and excited, Loesch set out to interview with the head of ABC's phone department.

The same day she got the call for the assistant cashier job, she also got a call from Ruth Avery at ABC saying she'd gotten the clerical job for the hardly astronomical salary of $350 a month. She listened to what her gut told her, turned down $1,000 a month, and took the ABC job. "I didn't know anything about TV. The father of the family I was staying with was horrified. Why did I do that? It was pure instinct. Something was telling me I better make a change."

As a side light to that story, Loesch never forgot Ruth Avery. When Loesch was president of Marvel Productions, she decided to write her a thank you letter. She told Avery, "You know it's because of you I'm now president of Marvel and if you hadn't seen something special in me, encouraged me, and given me that break I probably wouldn't be where I am today. I'll never forget you. I so appreciate what you did."

Avery wrote Loesch back. The note said, "Dear Margaret, I don't really remember you. But, I'm so pleased. . . ." Then it hit Loesch, Ruth Avery probably told everybody that there was something special about them. "I thought she meant it to me," Loesch said. "I envisioned that every time she read about me in the newspaper, she'd cry, and she didn't even remember me. It kind of put me in my place."

Loesch rarely forgets her place. Five years from that phone department job in 1971, she was a production manager in ABC's film department. Then NBC lured her away to run their Saturday morning children's shows. She knew nothing about children's television, but she felt it would be a good move. As vice president of children's television, Loesch moved NBC to the number one place in children's TV.

After four years, Joe Barbera brought her to Hanna-Barbera, then the top kidvid producers in the business. Loesch would return to NBC shortly thereafter and sell her protégé, Phyllis Tucker Vinson, a little show for children based on a village of tiny blue characters. The rest is Smurf history.

With her success at Hanna-Barbera, Loesch was settling into

her role as H-B's resident development genius. "I was so comfortable at H-B. I had a wonderful position and no complaints." Then another chance came her way. Marvel Productions, a subsidiary of the famed Marvel Comics and the creations of Stan Lee—with *Flash Gordon*, *Captain America*, *Mandrake the Magician*, and *Spiderman*—was looking for a new president, and they wanted Loesch. The job meant a cut in pay, a smaller, less well known company, and less credibility. Her intuition began speaking to her loud and clear.

As she was weighing the possibilities, her secretary, Barbara Song, came into her office and said, "Margaret, comfort doesn't mean growth." She turned around and walked out. Every reason Loesch could think of was telling her she shouldn't take the job. Reason had nothing to do with it. She listened to her intuition and took the job at Marvel. Within two years, Loesch had tripled Marvel's gross earnings and had catapulted it into the top three animation houses in the country. She did it in part with some help from some more little friends, Jim Henson's *Muppet Babies*. In her first year, Marvel won three Emmys. Loesch was hot.

Then came the deal. It was a real storybook tale. Disney, the king of animation, from *Snow White* to *Beauty and the Beast*, was coming to Marvel for help in TV animation. If ever there was a match made in cartoon heaven, here it was. Loesch's reaction was the same. It was so obvious.

Loesch ushered the Disney execs into her chic, modern office. The walls were painted a comfortable gray, and the chairs and sofa gave the office a feeling of a rounded quality. There were no sharp edges. The lights were tastefully, but appropriately, low—understated with a sense of elegance, just like Margaret herself.

The negotiations began. Disney laid out their position. Having never been involved in producing television animation, they came to Marvel because they had the television production expertise. Disney had the money and the ideas. Together they would join in a co-venture. It was a wonderful opportunity. As Loesch described it, "I could feel success." Talk about instant credibility.

All of a sudden there were the headlines across the trades and major newspapers, "Marvel and Disney co-venture!" "Disney on TV with Marvel!" Loesch now could walk into any network office and sell shows just by saying good morning. The co-venture would bring money and product into the company. It would facilitate a number of network deals. Disney *needed* Marvel. Loesch knew that Marvel and Disney could work together. She also knew that too many egos would not work well in this situation, but she had a strong sense of herself, and decided that wouldn't be a problem.

As negotiations progressed, Loesch could see that Marvel was involved in these discussions for all the right reasons. But some new information she was getting from Disney started to go against her initial instinct.

"I can remember the day I made that decision," Loesch said."I felt trepidation. I was nervous. I was worried. But I also had a sense of real calm. I walked away from the deal. I made a decision that ultimately what they wanted was not in the best interest of my company, even though I knew politically it would be wonderful. It didn't fit in with the long-range goals of Marvel. The short range was fantastic, but in the long range we would probably be diminished by Disney, and we would be helping to create and establish new credibility for Disney at our expense."

Her nervousness that day, though, did not have to do with whether she was making the right decision. It came from having to make the call to the corporate heads in New York. She had to tell them that she was saying "no" to Disney and listen to them scream "Margaret, are you out of your mind?" Meanwhile, the networks would be saying, "Are you crazy, Margaret, you passed up Disney?" She had heard those voices questioning her intuition before. As she made that call back east, her calm came from her personal conviction that she was absolutely right. It overrode her nervousness. This was a decision in which all the style and empty rounded chairs in her presidential office couldn't help her make. It was hers alone.

Disney eventually got into children's TV with another animation house. Both her corporation and the networks thought she was nuts, but they began to see. As the relationship between Disney and their partner began to develop, it became clear that Loesch's intuitive sense of the potential had been absolutely flawless.

"When I make a decision," Loesch says, feeling the strength of successful decisions behind her, "I have to think in terms of does this decision fit into whatever long-range plan I have for the company. Generally, in TV, a lot of decision making has very little to do with long-range strategies and more to do with Band-Aids and deadlines." It is fire-fighting, reactive mentality which destroys creative vision. There is no time to sit and ponder the future. Not only that, for many TV executives, the average job length is about two years. The attitude becomes, "Why make long-range plans when a few months down the road you'll be working for someone else?"

That is not the case with Loesch. She has a clear sense of where she wants her company to be in one year, three years, and five years. "I have to be sure I pull myself back on the day-to-day process, and say, wait a minute, am I getting bogged down? I still want to achieve 'X' in five years. What do I do today to get me closer to that goal?"

There's another important factor in Loesch's decision-making process, her willingness to make a mistake. "That willingness to make mistakes, diminishes the mistakes I make."

As Dr. Joseph Wheelwright makes clear, "Intuition is by no means 100 percent right, even if you've got a very well-developed one. It needs to be checked. If you don't check your intuition you're asking for trouble, and you're sure as hell going to get it."

Mistakes plague everyone. No one is above making a bad call, misjudging an unexpected curve, or just plain misreading the signs. But as frustrating as it may seem (surely there could be an easier, less harsh way), we do learn from our mistakes. Not too surprisingly, how we adjust and recover from our miscues eventually plays a significant role in determining our future successes.

The reasons for these mistakes are as varied as the decisions that have determined them. For the intuitive decision maker like Loesch, there invariably comes a time when a decision demands to be made and her intuitive prowess seems to have flown the coop. Her most tried and trusted sense has gone, left no forwarding address, and no date for its projected return. "You try to be logical, take everything you've heard, and think it through. If I do this, that will happen. If I do that, this will happen."

These can be crushing times for a decision maker. Decisions start going wrong, and no matter how hard you pull on the reins there seems to be no response. As the Mark Taper Forum's Gordon Davidson explains it, "I don't think that the intuition goes off as much as the execution of what it is you think you want to do gets screwed up. This can happen either by circumstance, lack of preparation, or a failure of imagination." There are many reasons for making errors, but when the technique you've always used suddenly abandons you, decisions can really go awry.

Robert Schoenberg believes that "a modest profusion of mistakes is actually a welcome sign of organizational health. You should be suspicious," he says in his book *The Art of Being a Boss*, "if no one in a group makes a mistake. If they never stumble, it is probably because they are standing still."

It's Schoenberg's contention that being wrong does wonderful things for the mind. It makes people realize they have to do something differently. They have to go back and reexamine the process. When things end badly, people retreat in earnest, which eventually leads to making better decisions. For the intuitive decision maker whose intuition has temporarily checked out, reexamining where the process broke down is extremely important if the intuitive function is to be trusted again.

Mistakes must also be viewed in context. Schoenberg recounts the story of a Pillsbury executive who was called into his boss's office after making a half-million-dollar mistake. Sitting there staring at his feet, the executive could feel the ax ready to fall. The boss started talking to him about new projects and new ideas. Suddenly the executive was confused. He looked up at his boss and asked, "Aren't you going to fire me?"

The boss snapped back. "Fire you? Hell, I just spent a half-million dollars educating you!" He was then sent to a three-day seminar called, "What We Just Learned About What We Should Never Do Again."

The Ford Motor Company's Edsel is probably the penultimate example in American business history where research, timing, and intuition flew out the window in unison. In a newspaper ad which appeared on "E-Day" 1957 (the day the Edsel was introduced to the world with more fanfare than had ever been seen before), Henry Ford II, the company's president, and Ernest R. Breech, the company's chairman, stood next to their new make with the pride and dignity of new fathers. The caption accompanying the ad explained how Ford himself had come to the decision to produce this innovative car. "Based on what we knew, guessed, felt, believed, suspected—about you, YOU are the reason behind the Edsel."

Two years later, on November 19, 1959, and $350 million lighter in the pocket, Ford discontinued production of its Edsel. *Time* magazine called it "The wrong car, for the wrong market, at the wrong time."

Ford may have known, guessed, felt, believed, and suspected certain things about his audience, but he was sure wrong. How could intuition have failed so badly? In spite of what the company claimed, their preparation was poor, their research late, and their execution pitiful. All the ingredients necessary for clear intuitive vision were clouded by the rosy glasses of false hopes and inadequate preparation. Though the Ford Company survived the Edsel debacle, as did those individuals personally involved with the decision making process, they probably all could have signed up for the Pillsbury seminar.

For Loesch, avoiding miscues and producing shows that will make it on TV demands an intuitive ability that combines all the timing, trend setting, negotiating, and luck a person can possibly muster. Television production is as crazy-making as it is profitable. If one element is out of kilter, everything crumbles. But then, that's show biz.

Loesch has seen these problems arise from both sides of the aisle. "You must be willing to accept the responsibility that the decision you make could be wrong," she says. "I always ask, 'What's the worst that could happen? Is somebody going to take a gun and kill me?' No. I have found that you tend to make less mistakes if you are willing to take a chance."

That doesn't mean she hasn't made mistakes. Loesch laughs when she remembers one of the poorest decisions she ever made in her life. "I sold my Volkswagen six weeks before the gas crisis. That was really stupid."

As Ray Brown says in *Judgment in Administration*, "People can be counted as statistics, but they can't be counted on to act like statistics. There is only a human way to handle human problems. This makes intuition an extremely valuable adjunct to an administrator's judgment." By working with the humanity of herself and her employees, Loesch can address the havoc often caused by mistakes, even when it was the temporary departure of intuition itself that may have caused the calamity.

Allowing for mistakes is essential to being both human and to making successful decisions. Of course, the perspective used to view mistakes is also important. As James Joyce said in *Ulysses*, "A man of genius makes no mistakes. His errors are volitional and are the portals of discovery." In other words, there are no problems, only challenges to improve. Intuition is not above improvement. Like practice in any field, the more one uses the process, the better one gets at it.

Trusting an untested creative answer demands a confidence in the feel of things. This is the emotional side of intuition. "Many times," Loesch says, "I feel I have to try and separate my quick, human, emotional instinct from my decisions. But then there are times when I say, damn it, I'm going to let my emotions out. Intuition for me is very emotional."

In this regard, Loesch feels women in business have a wonderful advantage. They are often closer to their emotions than men. "What is business but a group of people working together? Going with your intuition allows your emotions to affect your decisions, so you are absolutely responding to everything you are getting in a very honest way.

"I think that anybody that becomes too analytical and too attached to the research data really loses something important. People. You have to be able to respond, and you have to be able to trust. And that is often very emotional and very intuitive."

Loesch also wants the people she works with to embody these intuitive qualities. "I look for someone who displays wisdom. For me, that's a combination of experience and an intuitive ability to solve problems. I definitely don't want anybody who just goes by the seat of his or her pants and won't do their homework. Especially in our business. People say, 'Oh I did it by the gut. Everything is by the gut.' I think that's shabby and shoddy executive behavior. I look for someone who has a general understanding of their craft, real knowledge and experience, combined with a gentility. I look for that wisdom, because those people can respond to just about any situation. They have an inner resource strength and flexibility that can resolve a situation."

Resolving difficult situations is not always a group effort. After all has been suggested, researched, reaffirmed, contradicted, restructured, and examined from one perspective and then another, over a period of time, the decision is often left to the boss. It's at times like these that Loesch has to get away from the office. Her favorite getaway is to go driving in her car. In Los Angeles, driving the crowded freeways may be an odd place for meditative reflection, but it's easy to slip on the auto-pilot and begin mulling things over. This is a time to simply allow the brain to process. It is also a time Loesch listens. She finds a similar space by just going for a walk. "I walk a couple of miles a day to keep my sanity," she says, "and it's during those times things become crystal clear to me. I can hear what my instincts are telling me. I have found it's very dangerous for me to lose touch with what my intuition tells me."

This has become especially true as president of a children's network. There was once a time when children's TV was the network's bastard step-child. It was something they had to do, but no one really put much stock into it. Today with cable and the emergence of Loesch's Fox and its highly aggressive and successful attack on the market, children's TV has become an incredibly competitive, extremely tough market. This constant battle doesn't always allow Loesch the opportunity to make the most popular decisions. She has to make the decisions she believes are right.

Her arrival at the Fox Children's Network was one of those decisions. "Coming to Fox was very traumatic for me. It was not a move I elicited." During her six years at Marvel, she had seen three different owners come and go. Increasingly, she found herself being called upon to justify Marvel's existence to bankers and buyers.

It was an extremely frustrating time for Loesch. She was being pulled away from production and forced to address the short-term goals of the various owners whose main interest was always to sell Marvel again. In spite of the company's turmoil, she was still trying to maintain the high quality of the product that had made Marvel so attractive a purchase in the first place. It was around this time that rumors of a Fox Children's Network began coalescing into fact. Loesch arranged a meeting with the President of the Fox Television Network, Jamie Kellner. As one of the top children's television producers in town, she wanted Marvel to sell their product to Fox.

It was during one of their continuing meetings that Kellner asked Loesch her opinion of a capable executive to head Fox. She offered a few choices, never even considering herself. She had a job she liked, one in which she was successful and comfortable. It never occurred to her to even suggest herself. It had occurred to Kellner, and he offered her the job. "Suddenly" she said, "I heard Barbara Song, 'Comfort doesn't mean growth.'"

Again, the choice meant less money, but this time the situation was different. Fox was a company that wanted to be in the children's business, and wanted her to be a creative executive. "We've got number crunchers," Kellner told her. "Just stick to the budget and you'll be responsible for designing the shows." It had been almost ten years since she left NBC.

She moved across town to Fox in March 1990. She had come from an organization where her time had been consumed with fighting fires. That situation was not what prompted her shift, however, because as she explains it, "At Fox, it was all fire. I came on in March and they wanted us on the air in September." By all industry standards, this was virtually impossible. Thirty minute animation shows require four months to produce. The directive was "Just get on the air."

Relying on her experience, her well-tuned instinct, and sheer hard work, Loesch and her crew accomplished the impossible. She also realized that to enter into the kid's TV market the same old thing was not going to make it. Loesch knew Fox couldn't be more of the same. Fox's first season included some of the zaniest most creative cartoons on TV. "Zazoo U" was created by poet Shane DeRolf, and shows like the incredibly popular "Bobby's World," "Beetlejuice," and "Tiny Toon Adventures" have made the Fox Children's Network the act to beat in children's TV. These were literally off-the-wall cartoons, and the kids loved them.

It's that willingness to be different, to trust the intuitive impulse, that has become a hallmark of Loesch's success. Her most recent stunning success at Fox was just such a move. Warner Brothers brought her a show, an animated drama, that Loesch's intuition told her would be huge. She received more negative feedback from affiliates and even people on her staff than any other program she has been involved with. They thought it would be too dark, too somber, too stylized, too dramatic. Loesch knew it was risky, but her instincts all pointed to it being the right kind of risky. The show was "Batman." And when it premiered on Fox in the fall of 1992, it exceeded even Loesch's expectations. It became the number one daily children's show on TV.

Loesch's experience has brought her back, time and again, to the notion that "comfort doesn't mean growth." And for her, growth is essential in becoming a better decision maker. "I've become more willing to listen, to follow that instinct, and get in touch with myself a little more. I have also developed an emerging philosophy that began when I worked at Hanna-Barbera with Peyo (creator of the Smurfs) and continued with Jim Henson (the Muppets). A singular person can make a difference. You must make sure that the visionary behind an idea gets his or her way, because it's never going to be right unless that person brings the idea to fruition." By knowing that in herself and recognizing it in others, Loesch has built a fledgling children's TV network into the leading innovator in the business. Beyond innovation, in less than three years Loesch has built Fox into what is undisputably the leading children's television network. Number one on Saturday morning—and number one Monday through Friday. This is a fact that pleases Margaret Loesch greatly.

As her colleagues point out, when it comes to children's television, "Margaret knows."

ROBERT PITTMAN
UNCONVENTIONALLY YOURS

The average man cannot contemplate such things as deeper processes of mind so long as "those who know" deny their existence.

JOSEPH CHILTON PEARCE

WHEN ROBERT PITTMAN created MTV, he was willing to know something others had yet to realize. He was willing to go against the conventional wisdom, because he knew he had an idea that would revolutionize the recording and television business. How did he know? "I spend a lot of time looking at macro issues— what's going on in the world," Pittman says from his twenty-seventh-floor office, high above Rockefeller Center in New York City. Sitting in his high-backed, black leather chair, behind his round marble-topped desk, he counsels, however that "research is not policy making. People make policy, research just answers some questions. At the end of the day, it's a gut decision."

At thirty-seven, Pittman is now CEO and president of Time Warner Enterprises and chairman and CEO of Six Flags Entertainment. Defying his youthful years, he lives his life racing from one success to the next. Pittman's climb to the heights above Radio

87

City Music Hall began when he was just fifteen and he landed his first gig as a part-time disk jockey in his native Mississippi.

He wears wire-rimmed glasses and has fresh, clean, corporate good looks—a marked contrast to his earlier bearded, long-hair hippie days. But his fondness for fast motorcycles, airplanes and helicopters, and climbing mountains, that require ropes, jumars, and carbineers keeps him firmly rooted in his youth. Pittman has built an empire on his connection to his youth and his conscious attack on the status quo.

The mid-seventies was a time when most people in Pittman's generation were finding themselves. Pittman found himself, by way of Jackson, Mississippi, Milwaukee, Wisconsin, Pittsburgh, Pennsylvania, and a country music radio station, WMAQ, in a not so country city, Chicago, Illinois. At this time in history, country music had moved out of the hollers, but had yet to make a big city impact. Pittman realized that the conventional wisdom that had always sold country music simply would not play in the Second City. The idea came to him—the whole picture. He figured that most of his potential audience was still listening to rock music instead of country. He decided to make WMAQ sound exactly like a Top 40 rock station except that he was going to play country music. He also brought the same big money giveaways featured on rock stations to WMAQ. The cry of "WMAQ's Gonna Make Me Rich!" was heard nonstop over Chicago's local TV stations. "The people in the country music business thought I was the anti-Christ, trying to destroy their industry," Pittman recalled. "But WMAQ became the number one country music station in America, and everyone started copying our format." In one rating period, WMAQ went from number 22 in the Chicago market to number 3.

With a pad of paper before him, a computer screen to his right, and three bookshelves behind him filled with video equipment, Pittman is ready to record any idea that comes to him. Tapping into his intuition is a matter of getting rid of the "hobgoblins of conventional thinking. You stop listening to the experts, to the way everyone says you should do it. If they're telling you how to do it, how come they haven't done it yet?

"I think conventional wisdom is a protector of the status quo. If you're going to shake it up, you have to put some radical approaches forward." For Pittman, business's biggest enemy is people saying, "It's not done that way." or "We've never done that before." It's an attitude that immediately inhibits creative thinking and problem solving. "I've never seen a solution to a problem come out of conventional wisdom," he says. "In almost every industry I know, the biggest breakthroughs come far afield of the conventional thinking."

Pittman is a full-fledged enemy of the status quo. He feels that people have a problem putting unusual ideas forward because they usually have to sell them to someone. Then the people they're selling it to go out and hire a consultant who looks at the prevailing market, (re: conventional wisdom) and they come back saying, "No, you can't do it that way." "If you're a functionary in an organization," Pittman says, "maybe the best thing you can do is say no, because you're not going to get in trouble. Unfortunately, what this does in a lot of organizations is to build a bias into their structures against innovation."

Pittman would find an ally in former California governor and three-time presidential candidate, Edmund G. "Jerry" Brown, Jr. "I think it is important to have a perspective, a view of the contemporary world," says Brown. "From that I derive my course of action. It becomes a criteria, an overall ecological sense that we are all part of a larger system and that we have to not only look out for our own particular well-being, but we have to perceive that well-being as tied up with the well-being of others. So we get a sense of wholeness. That is the goal.

"Now, how you apply that is to bring in a diversity of people. And, of course, in that process you are going to get conflicts. You are going to get misunderstanding. You are going to get a superficial sense of incoherence when some of the older patterns are being challenged, because they are not working for all the people in society."

So how does Pittman go about breaking the desire to hold onto the safe, tried, and true? Like Brown did in California, he establishes a culture and an environment conducive to creativity and innovation, one that honors the intuitive. "A tremendous number of great solutions come from ideas first spoken as a joke. Something is said that makes everyone laugh, and then you take a second look, and there's something there. That germ of an idea might end up being the perfect solution to a devastating problem. If it had been simply laughed off as a ridiculous idea, that creative solution might have been lost forever."

Gordon Davidson, the artistic director at the Mark Taper Forum in Los Angeles, refers to openness to creative and intuitive responses as the "primary fuse of ideas. Everything else happens after that hot journey down the fuse."

Pittman wants to encourage his people to light that fuse. "I want people to really talk about things and never feel like they'll be ridiculed for throwing out an unusual idea."

Brainstorming, when done properly, is a very powerful method of activating what people know. Doing it right means not censoring any ideas that are brought forward, writing down every response without comment, acknowledging people's contributions, and encouraging and unleashing the creative power of everyone present. In either a group or individual process, brainstorming can unlock a person's initial inner process. Facilitating this process in an organization requires an atmosphere where people feel comfortable to utilize the full extent of their intuitive and imaginative capabilities. He credits Steven J. Ross, Time Warner's late chairman and CEO, with the creation of this environment. "It's part of our culture here," Pittman says. "No one's going to be fired for making a mistake, because if you're not making mistakes, it means that you're not trying anything new."

Pittman recalls meetings he's been in with other executives whose subordinates have said, "We've got this great idea." Before they've gotten it out of their mouths, the executive has said, "It'll never work." Moments like these make him cringe. As a leader, he believes he has to find a way to stop that executive from saying,

"It'll never work." For Pittman, the creative process and the analytical process are two completely separate systems that shouldn't be mixed. "Let's consider how it might work before we say it won't work. Let's come to 'it won't work' as an absolute last resort." The trick Pittman believes is to get people to state their objections without making conclusions. How do we make this idea work with our pricing structure? Or how do we get people to be aware of this idea? These may raise someone's objections to an idea, but then people can respond to them. People have no way to respond to a conclusion such as, "It'll never work."

"We're all looking at ideas," Pittman says. "They may be weird ideas. Sometimes we may not know if they'll work. We just have to take a chance. I hope in my management I can continue that so we can keep moving forward constantly."

Making weird ideas incredibly successful has been Pittman's forte. In 1979 Pittman joined Warner Amex Satellite Entertainment to develop The Movie Channel. In 1981, as head of programming, he took a look around at the macro world and allowed his intuition to guide him. As Carl Jung stated, intuition is our ability to perceive possibilities—to see the global picture while addressing the local situation.

What Pittman saw was a generation of young people that had grown up loving television and rock music. Pittman also realized that rock music was not just entertainment for many young people; it was cultural identity. They established who they were by the music they listened to. "Go to a concert, no matter who it is," Pittman suggests, "and most of the audience looks the same. They're dressed alike because the artist represents a unifying factor for their culture. Heavy metal kids are all going to have torn-up blue jeans, jackets, long scraggly hair, and be mostly male. Rap is the urban equivalent of heavy metal. They all signify something.

"Understanding that, we set out with MTV to marry rock music and TV. The mistake people had made in this area in the past was that they tried to make music fit the form of TV. Television is basically a narrative form with a story arc. What we knew was that for music to succeed in this medium, we had to change the form of TV to match the music.

"We needed a defining attitude for the product, an umbrella under which everything would hang. We would define that attitude with our graphic look, our promotions, the balance of music we played, and our advertising. That's what made it unusual, different, and successful." Music videos weren't new. They'd been produced for the past three or four years. According to Pittman, "No one could crack the code and figure out how to make it successful." That is, of course until he nailed down his target.

What Pittman had done was demonstrate an innate sense of leadership. Something immediately recognizable by those higher up. James MacGregor Burns writes in his monumental book, *Leadership*, that in order to be an effective leader it is necessary to be able to communicate with people of widely different backgrounds, temperaments, interests, and attitudes. He notes, "The key elements in the process may be neither the message nor the medium, but the source and the target."

The conventional wisdom regarding MTV was that Pittman was crazy. First, there was a question as to whether the cable industry would succeed. Second, it wasn't certain that advertisers would buy advertising on it. As Pittman points out, "There is a rule in the advertising business that you don't buy national advertising unless the program has at least a 'three' national rating and covers seventy percent of the country. No one in cable does that even today." Pittman and his people had to rewrite how advertising was bought on TV, and they had to convince the record industry that by investing in music videos they would sell more records.

The genesis of MTV was a completely intuitive decision for Pittman. It was suddenly so obvious. "I was twenty-seven years old. I was so naive, I knew it would work." He pauses briefly, reflecting on the risky path he followed ten years earlier. "I think if I started it today, I might have some questions. We had a lot of barriers we had to knock down to succeed." Knocking down those barriers took incredible leadership; in the parlance of Marshall McLuhan, Pittman had to deliver the message, sell the medium, identify the source, and hit the target. With MTV, his aim was perfect.

Rallying people around his idea and making it a success required more than just a winning concept—it required leadership. On the wall in Pittman's office are photographs of him with Presidents Reagan and Bush. But the president with whom he might be more philosophically aligned is Franklin Roosevelt. Burns points out that Roosevelt had a keen intuitive grasp of the needs and motivation of his cabinet members and agency chiefs. Burns writes, "One of his many techniques—difficult for a man who loved to talk and dominate the scene—was simply to listen sympathetically to those who poured out their woes and frustrations (often caused by the President himself). He knew how to persuade one person by argument, another by charm, another by a display of self-confidence, another by flattery, another by an encyclopedic knowledge." Pittman's long-time radio mentor, Charlie Warner, would undoubtedly agree that Pittman possesses those qualities. In a 1989 article in *Gentleman's Quarterly*, Warner said, "[Pittman] has one of those very rare minds that is both analytical and creative." It was evident in 1972 when Warner hooked up with Pittman in Pittsburgh. "Even then," Warner adds, "he knew how to win."

Pittman is a great believer in action, in making the quick decision. In fact, he hasn't found any qualitative or quantitative difference in making a decision quickly or over a long period of time. What he has found is, "If you take a long time to make a decision and you make the wrong decision, it will take you a long time to get off that horse. It's the wrong decision that stays in place too long that creates the real problem." He finds that if an organization has a bias toward making quick decisions, it can quickly recognize mistakes and change.

This fast paced, pull-out-all-the-stops approach is the basis of Pittman's philosophy—if we've got to move, let's move. Let's not sit here and study things to death. This habit is known in many organizations as paralysis through analysis. Acting quickly on good information is extremely important, because, as stated earlier, unlike fine wine, good information does not age well. As Chrysler Corporation's former president Lee Iacocca says, "If you wait, by the time you act, your facts will be out of date because the market has moved on. . . . At some point, you have to take the leap of faith. First, because even the right decision is wrong if it's made too late. And second, in most things there is no such thing as certainty."

Even deadlier for an organization is having people in the organization knowingly defend wrong decisions. This often happens because these people are certain they'll be crucified for making a wrong decision. As Pittman reiterates, "It goes back to the trust in an organization that wrong decisions don't mean you're the wrong person."

As Margaret Loesch has said, "The more willing you are to make a mistake, the less mistakes you make." This is true individually and organizationally. Pittman has certainly proved both true.

If you're barely thirty and you've got one of the most successful new TV concepts on the air, where do you go? Time Warner gave Pittman Nickelodeon. When Pittman came on board, this floundering children's network was known within the business as the "spinach channel." It was approved by the PTA, endorsed by the National Educators Association, loved by parents—and hated by the kids—a miserable failure.

Pittman realized that what had worked with MTV, creating an attitude that reflected its audience, would work with Nickelodeon, too. He began speaking with people within the organization and found Gerry Laybourne, a woman in charge of program acquisition, whose sense of the unconventional jibed with Pittman's. "I think my intuition gets better the more I know. But to me everything is intuition, especially people decisions. We lie to each other when we say I picked that person because she's really smart or had the right answers. That's baloney. Someone walks into the room and you're either taken with them or you're not. Often, you're forming opinions before they open their mouth."

Pittman intuitively recognized that Laybourne was a kindred spirit. He put her in charge of figuring out what got kids excited and then put together a channel that reflected their attitudes and perspectives. As she radicalized the visual images and content of Nickelodeon, she lost some parents, educators, and PTA presidents, but she brought in the kid viewers by the eyeful. Nickelodeon threw out the spinach, literally brought in green, gooey slime, and the ratings numbers oozed up. It was all because the presentation and attitude Laybourne created for Nickelodeon reflected its viewers. Its success has spawned many imitators throughout the children's TV business.

Pittman wasn't done with Nickelodeon. Every night at eight o'clock, Nickelodeon went off the air and the transponder was rented to the Arts & Entertainment channel. Pittman set to work. It was Nickelodeon's transponder, and he felt they could do something on Nickelodeon that would be worth more than the $1.5 million in rent Arts & Entertainment paid.

They came up with an idea based on the attitudes of a different generation—one that had grown up on "Leave it to Beaver," "The Donna Reed Show," "Oh, Susannah," and "Car 54 Where are You?" At the time, these baby boomers were actively sitting around with friends playing TV trivia. What was the theme song to Donna Reed? I can see her coming down the stairs, handing out the lunches. Or what was the name of the dog in "My Three Sons"? Pittman and his colleagues' idea was to take all these old shows and instead of taking them seriously, put them on a channel that would spoof TV. They called it "TV for the TV Generation." Thus was born "Nick at Night." It cost them half a million dollars a year to put on the air. The advertising dollars flowed in at a vastly greater rate.

If imitation is the highest form of flattery, what is it called when you imitate your own accomplishments? That's exactly what Pittman ended up doing thanks to a competitor of some note, Ted Turner. Turner decided to take on MTV and launch a video music station of his own. His intent was to fragment MTV's audience. Pittman and crew brainstormed. If there's room for

Turner, they conjectured, then there's obviously room for another music video network. We should be able to do it cheaper, because we can do it at an incremental cost, tagging it on to MTV. That was the birth of VH-1.

Turner initially signed up around 400,000 subscribers for his station, while VH-1 landed two million. Turner shut down thirty-four days later.

As CEO of Time Warner Enterprises, Pittman is responsible for the strategic business and development unit of Time Warner Inc. This unit is in charge of creating or acquiring assets that will utilize the full range of Time Warner properties. One of his major projects has been the acquisition and restructuring of the "Six Flags" theme parks.

Once again, it was by taking a look at the global picture, by realizing what changes would be taking place in the consumer's behavior, that Pittman discovered this new opportunity. In the late 1980s Pittman and his people began focusing on what the 1990s were going to be about. Pittman had already learned that the baby boomers set the tone for the country. And the boomers had spent a good deal of time in the 1980s having families. With that knowl-edge, Pittman returned to his proven approach.

"Theme parks are the perfect family entertainment out of the home." The Six Flags parks are all large scale facilities scattered from one end of the country to the other. In doing his research, Pittman discovered what he believes is a hidden asset in the parks. Six Flags parks had never been made into a national brand. Sud-denly, Pittman is facing off head-to-head with Disney, initiating a $30 million ad campaign proclaiming that Six Flags parks are "big-ger, faster, and closer" than Disney's, all of which happens to be true. For example, Disneyland's Space Mountain clocks in at 35 mph. Six Flags's Shock Wave roller coaster screams by at an aver-age speed of 65 mph. Pittman's intuition paid off again. In 1992, the first year under Pittman, Six Flags had record profits despite the lingering recession.

Pittman has always taken over businesses that were doing

poorly or just starting up, and his decisions have always taken a radical departure. "Every decision I make is a gut decision."

With Six Flags going strong, Pittman is now casting his gaze toward the future, which is carrying him into the world of interactive television. His theory is one based on experience and a keen grasp of what he knows. "The reason the TV business was a boom business in the seventies and eighties was the fact that all of us who had grown up with TV in our households became adults and took the habit with us. When you introduce technology into someone's life, you must introduce it into a life where they are learning about the world, which means five- , six- , and seven-year-olds. If you try and introduce new technology to someone my age, it's always an add-on. It never becomes totally integrated. What we saw in the TV business was the emergence of TV babies. We didn't want four channels; we wanted a hundred and fifty. If you asked my parents, do you want cable TV, they'll say, 'Honey I can't even watch those four channels I have now.' You ask me, and I say 'You bet!' The next generation behind us are the computer babies, who grew-up with VCRs and Nintendo sets. To them, that is TV."

With that picture in mind, Pittman proceeded forward. "The next big industry using the TV," he says referring to a picture of his young son before him, "is the world of random access TV. TV you can control and move around."

Pittman calls this process of decision making "the big think." These ideas may come to him when he least expects it; when he is zooming down the highway on his motorcycle, taking a shower, or simply lying in bed. "I can't tell you the number of times I've hopped up in the middle of the night, an idea flashes in my head and I have to write it down. These things are often so fleeting, it'll leave me if I don't get it down. Once I do, I can edit the idea, improve upon it, and enhance it." The fuse is lit.

Pittman travels with his pad, and once a week he rewrites what's on it. He does this even if nothing has changed from the time he originally wrote it down. This allows him to focus on each point again and keep them fresh in his mind. He goes over his list before staff meetings, before meetings with executives, or whenever he's alone for a few minutes. By keeping these problems, ideas, and issues close at hand, he is constantly priming his intuition to offer a solution. And he listens, no matter the time, no matter the place. He's prepared for an answer. "When you get an idea, listen to it."

He applies this same intuitive process when dealing with people. "I think it's very important, if you are the kind of leader who has a great respect for other people, to understand who they are and what they need, so that you can serve their needs. It's unrealistic to expect people to work for you if they're not getting some psychic income, some sense of self-satisfaction, and some self reward from what they are doing." Part of Pittman's responsibility as CEO of Time Warner Enterprises is to make sure that his people are getting those regular doses of psychic income. As a manager, intuiting that need is vital because it's often a far more valuable compensation than money.

Kazuo Inamori, founder of Kyoto Ceramics, would find Pittman's philosophy encouraging. "I think there is one thing that American businessmen can learn by studying Japanese businessmen," he says. "The Japanese businessmen manage by valuing the heart."

Recognizing and bestowing those inner payback rewards on colleagues and employees brings tremendous results. People want to deliver for someone who gives them all the creative freedom they require. Too often companies keep their employees on short leashes. Leaders don't only lead by directive, they lead by example. It's no wonder then that the respect, creativity, and success inspired by Pittman's own inner processes have propelled him to the top of Time Warner's corporate chart at the age of thirty-seven. Fueled by the power of the unconventional, Pittman inevitably trusts his gut.

HAROLD WILLIAMS

THE BUSINESS OF OIL
AND PAINTINGS

One ought to see everything that one has a chance of seeing; because in life not many have one chance and none has
two.

SARD HARKER

WHEN HAROLD WILLIAMS left his chairmanship of the Securities
and Exchange Commission to become president of the J. Paul
Getty Trust, he was being brought in to oversee the wealthiest art
organization since the Medicis'. It was a challenge he welcomed.

Just off the Pacific Coast Highway in Malibu, California,
stands the J. Paul Getty Museum. Faithfully recreated from the
plans of the Villa de Papiri in Herculaneum (the original was
destroyed in the gigantic eruption of Mount Vesuvius that also
buried Pompeii), the museum sits quietly and unobtrusively.

Running this trust fund was a task Williams instinctively
wanted. The fund's primary investment purpose was to buy art
for its museum, an area in which Williams had little experience.

Williams is a quick study, however; Norton Simon, who years earlier had made Williams chairman of his organization, had said that
by the time Williams was twenty-six he "knew more about tax law
than most senior lawyers and more about accounting than anybody on our accounting staff."

Today the J. Paul Getty Trust Fund is worth $3.9 billion—the
world's richest trust fund. At sixty-four, Williams has grown to
trust his "gut" feeling when it comes to decisions, learning early in
his business career from a master—industrialist and advertising
magnate Norton Simon. He credits Simon, whom he describes as
"an incredibly bright man with incredible instincts," with having
more of an impact on his personal growth than anyone else.

This former chairman of the Securities and Exchange Commission and former dean and professor of management of the Graduate School of Management at the University of California, Los
Angeles, remembers a phone conversation with Simon that after
thirty years still stays with him. Williams was in his early thirties
and in Simon's employ. Simon was facing a very difficult problem,
which Williams believed he could solve. He told Simon what he
thought he ought to do.

There was silence on the other end of the phone. Williams listened. Then the man said in a soft, broken voice, "Harold you
can't imagine how alone I feel."

Williams's response was immediate. "Sure I can." But he had
little idea what Simon meant. It wasn't until years later, when
Williams himself was in charge that he began to understand the
loneliness of the decisive leap. The only tool a decision maker has
at that moment is his or her intuition and sense of self.

The courage to make the decisional leap is found in that lonely
place where no further input can be either added or detracted.
Only action can be taken. This is the place that separates those
who succeed from those who maintain. Michael Maccoby calls the
latter "careerists." They are the ones who try to get through by following the safest path. These are people whose decisions are
based not on a sense of vocation, but solely on a sense of career.
Careerism, "results not only in constant anxiety," Maccoby says,

"but also in an underdeveloped heart. Overly concerned with adapting himself to others, to marketing himself, the careerist constantly betrays himself, since he must ignore idealistic, compassionate, and courageous impulses that might jeopardize his career."

This was never Williams's pattern. One time Williams blithely offered Simon a suggestion. Simon asked him why he liked it, and Williams replied, "It's just my sense of it."

Simon didn't want to offend the young Williams, but he did say, "You know, Harold, if anyone is going to run this company by the seat of his pants, he's going to do it by the seat of *my* pants."

After leaving Simon's company, he traveled back to his alma mater, UCLA, to become dean of the School of Business. By the time Williams left to become chairman of the SEC seven years later, he had raised UCLA's business school from one among many to one of the best.

Williams obviously knew how to function in the worlds of business, education, politics, and money. Moving in to manage what started out as a $700 million trust fund for a museum was something he knew something about, but the deciding factor was that the job also offered a new and exciting challenge: He would learn about a world where passion often overrules prudence, the art world. Little did he know that the job of president of the Getty Trust was going to be more like playing a starring role on a television soap opera than merely being the respected leader of the world's richest museum. Nor did he figure on being the catalyst for what would eventually be one of the largest and most controversial corporate takeovers in American history. It would eventually raise the coffers of his trust fund from around $700 million to some $3.9 billion.

This was the fourth major career move he made of his own volition in a career that had taken him from a law firm in Los Angeles to Norton Simon's companies to UCLA to the Securities and Exchange Commission and now to the J. Paul Getty Trust. He trusted the internal clock inside him that said, "It's time for a change." He recalls when he told his friend, the distinguished Norman Cousins, how his internal clock was pushing him to accept UCLA's offer, even though it meant taking an 80 percent cut in salary. Cousins cautioned him, "Harold, there are times when the wheel only turns once."

Eleven years later, before his SEC position was to end, he followed his instincts again. He accepted the chairmanship of the Getty Trust after being highly recommended by Franklin D. Murphy, former chancellor of UCLA. He wrote to Norman Cousins, "The wheel just turned again."

Williams had no idea where that wheel would ultimately deliver him. He found himself in a drama in which the cast of characters were all major players. There was Gordon P. Getty, son of the late J. Paul Getty, and now the richest man in America. He was sole trustee of the family fortune and controlled 40 percent of Getty Oil stock. Second was Sidney R. Petersen, chairman of Getty Oil. Third was Williams, who controlled 12 percent of Getty stock, the second largest holding.

It was no secret that Gordon Getty was feuding with Getty management. He was against diversification into insurance and cable TV. His real interests, however, were music and opera, not business, but he soon began singing a different tune. Gossip circulated about dissent at Getty board meetings.

Most stock analysts were aware that Getty stock had been undervalued for quite some time. Williams also knew, but what was he to do about it? Petersen had begun to seek alternatives, one possibility being to issue more shares, thereby diluting the combined power of Gordon Getty and the museum. This suggestion provoked Gordon, who decided he wanted to seize more power in the company. Management opposed him. Getty turned to Harold Williams for help. "Together," he told Williams, "we can oust the Getty management." Williams was said to have branded this idea as outrageous!

The battle raged on between Getty and management, each trying to outfox the other. In stepped Harold Williams.

Out of his vast experience, he realized that the first thing to do was impose a cooling-off period. Williams had become rightfully concerned about his trust. By law, he had to divest the trust of its stock, but with all the infighting he feared it might attract a hostile takeover offer. The trust might not benefit enough from this kind of takeover. Williams prevailed upon Gordon Getty and management to sign what would be called the "tripartite agreement." It was, in essence, a declaration of a one-year truce.

Unfortunately there were too many holes in it, and the truce lasted all of one month. Petersen started working on J. Paul Getty, Jr., the reclusive son of the oil magnate who had been living on a "small inheritance" and had no corporate role. The idea was for J. Paul Jr. to contest Gordon's sole control of the family trust and then have a cotrustee appointed over the trust.

As Williams recalls, "My intuition told me this was the time to turn." He was furious with management's actions. Petersen had misled both Getty and Williams. He told Gordon that now was the time to act. Together, they assumed legal command of the company. It was a decision that would set into motion a series of events with a timing that proved absolutely astounding.

First Gordon and Williams had to revise the firm's bylaws to reduce Petersen's power. In the suit brought by management on behalf of J. Paul Jr., Gordon's attorneys raised the question of J. Paul's mental health and accused the company officials of coercing J. Paul into actions, "whose consequences he may not have appreciated."

In the meantime, Getty stock had begun to rise. Wall Street smelled an acquisition. Getty Oil rose fourteen points to over $72 a share. Then Pennzoil entered the fray. Pennzoil's chairman, the burly, tough-minded J. Hugh Liedtke, struck a deal with Gordon to initiate a leveraged buyout of the Getty management that would give Pennzoil 43 percent of the company and Gordon 57 percent. The price Pennzoil was offering was $110 a share, or $5.3 billion for the 60 percent of the stock not controlled by Gordon Getty.

The proposal was presented to the Getty board and rejected. The board felt the company was worth more. Later that day Gordon and Liedtke came back with an offer of $112.50 a share. The investment bankers representing both the museum and Gordon Getty told the board that this was the best price the stock could command. The deal was reluctantly approved. Liedtke and Gordon Getty thought they had pulled it off, but the series of events Williams had set in motion had not yet played out.

Before Williams could sell the trust's shares, he had to get the approval of his board of directors. Then a niece, another beneficiary of the trust under Gordon's control, secured a court order blocking the sale until all the facts were presented to the beneficiaries. As *Fortune* magazine's Peter Nulty described the situation, "Liedtke and Gordon had 'teed' the company up, as dealmakers say, by making the first offer. But while the restraining order was in force, a new player was free to step up and hit the ball."

Up stepped Texaco's John McKinley. He had directed First Boston, his investment bank, to come up with a manageable purchase price for Getty. They returned with an offer of $125 a share. Whom did they seek out first? Harold Williams.

Williams immediately agreed to sell the trust's 12 percent to Texaco. Then Texaco descended upon Gordon Getty with an open hand. It didn't take much for him to assess Texaco's strength with the museum trust shares already in their pocket and the potential to control 60 percent of the company. He played his only real option and became a full partner in the deal.

It was a good idea. The company sold for a reported $9.9 billion. Williams's intuitive decision to initially back Gordon Getty, which he later admitted "was a real high risk," had released the flood gates. The museum trust now had tripled its endowment up from $700 million to $2.2 billion. Gordon Getty was even richer. Even Pennzoil, which seemed to bear the brunt of the transaction, eventually benefited.

Williams has always had a knack for making the right moves at the right time. They are usually moves that put his organization, in this case the Getty Trust, in the right light. For example, within moments of the time that L.A.'s architecturally renowned downtown public library was engulfed in flames on April 29, 1986, Williams was on the phone to Mayor Tom Bradley offering financial help. The following week, he publicly offered a $2 million gift from the Getty Trust. McDonnell Douglas, IBM, and Arco later offered help, but the Getty Trust was the first on the scene. It was an offer that did wonders for the museum's image at a time when the trust needed public acceptance and approval. The new Getty Art Center was soon to be constructed in the hills behind Brentwood. Not just a few attractive buildings, mind you, but 24 acres of buildings surrounded by 742 acres of choice terrain with an expansive view of Los Angeles. This land had originally been slated to be a wildlife preserve. This "paving the way" was the kind of action that was expected from Williams when he was named president of the Getty Trust.

Williams was sincerely concerned about the terribly destructive library fire, but his mind told him that there was no better way to show the city that Getty was committed to be an important part of it. It could be called intuition, and it could be called a strong desire to help. Whichever it was, the city and Getty Museum both stand as winners. At the time of his appointment to the Getty post, many art professionals, art curators, and historians around the country raised their eyebrows at the Getty Trust's decision. But they soon, and some begrudgingly, agreed that he was the man for the job. Williams possessed the insight, an immense appreciation for the arts, and the intuitive business sense needed to oversee the enormously challenging job of putting the institution's substantial resources to their most effective use.

In 1981 the trust began a year-long investigation with the goal of developing a responsible overall plan. Williams said, "The result of the investigation was the decision to focus the trust on three under-supported areas—scholarship, education, and conservation—in addition to continuing to selectively build the museum collection." He also emphasized that, "The primary purpose of the Getty Trust is to create and operate its own programs, in contrast to foundations that fund the programs of others."

There is, as Williams pointed out, a limit to what the Trust can spend. According to new laws, it is limited to spending no more than 4.25 percent of the value of the endowment. Anything beyond that must be reinvested.

Williams is now focused on trying to allay the concerns of people in the art community (artists and art collectors), museums, and critics who fear that the Getty Trust will wreck the delicate balance in art acquisitions. He decided that since it is theoretically true that if the trust really wants something, it can get it, the trust will always be a responsible competitor. Williams sets limits on what they think a piece of art is worth and what the trust is willing to pay for it. He said, "We have lost pieces of art to others because of that."

As far as the arts generally are concerned, Williams believes that awareness and education may be the best answer. One of his goals is to dispel the mind-sets of some people when it comes to art—that it is only an elite creative activity or only a therapeutic activity. He believes that by "developing a good substantive program for the education of the arts" school districts can keep the arts vital, alive, and growing within their curriculum. As Williams puts it, "You don't have a civilization without the arts." He concedes that technology and science are powerful forces, but "alone [don't] make a civilization." He is also looking at areas of communication and education for people who are not in school. He believes most of what is available today is quite ineffectual. He notes, referring to museums, "What museums do in the field of educating and informing people once they come into a museum is not as strong as it could be." He doesn't have the answer yet, but he's exploring ways to do it better.

Williams makes a practice of making three or four speeches every year on substantial issues—not all related to the art field. "I know what has been said and talked about on an issue," he says, "so I take it to the next step and then add something. What I'm looking for are alternative positions and contributions. That's basically the way researchers tend to work and should work." He acknowledges that the Getty Trust is in the unique position of being able to try different approaches in arts education. "It's an undertaking only an institution like ours could take on," he said. "We don't have to succeed in everything. We don't have to be popular. Government needs to worry that it is perceived as being all things to all people. We don't have to stand for election publicly every two years."

Williams is serious about what he's doing. He's excited about what he's doing. He sees the Getty fund as a way to make an impact on our culture and education—with a special emphasis on art appreciation. As he said in a *New York Times* interview, "Part of the yeast of this place is that it represents diverse points of view. There's a freedom in each of our activities that's very different from what would be under the umbrella of the museum."

In a speech Williams gave in November 1992 on "Arts and Educational Excellence," he referred to the 1983 publication by the United States Department of Education, "A Nation at Risk," which concluded that America's children were being poorly educated. He lamented, "The situation has not improved much in the years since." He discussed the problems that exist in American education today and said, "To meet that challenge our schools must prepare young people not just to be efficient workers, but also to be creative and critical thinkers. At issue is not merely a few hours in the school week, but rather a fundamental belief about what America's children need to know."

Williams is a strong believer in taking risks to further the trust's goals. Fortunately, the trust can afford to do it and has been pretty successful at it. As he put it, "I believe that the Getty's commitment, though finite, can begin to make a difference. Great art is one of the most profound and enduring achievements of mankind. Its presence enriches our lives and the humaneness of our society. As the visual record of history, art also helps us to understand the values and forces that have shaped this and other civilizations. Through its programs, the J. Paul Getty Trust should contribute to this enrichment and understanding."

Backing up those words, the Getty is currently sponsoring a project in Egypt, which is monitoring environmental effects on the Great Sphinx at Giza. For Williams, exhilaration comes from new challenges. In each life move he has made, he has taken on something he has never done before and excelled. His intuition has been a key ingredient in his success, a success he bases on three important ingredients—"experience, knowing yourself, and being comfortable being alone"—the essence of intuition.

PETER H. DAILEY

THE MAKER OF PRESIDENTS

In order to survive, we must break tradition.

WALT GODDARD

ON A GLORIOUS Washington spring day in 1970, the cherry blossoms having barely fallen to the ground, Peter Dailey, president of Dailey and Associates advertising, was offered the prestigious—and profitable—opportunity to run President Nixon's media reelection campaign. When he walked into his first meeting with former Attorney General John Mitchell and Maurice Stans, who headed the Committee to Reelect the President (CREEP), Dailey knew he had entered the door of power. They spoke to him about their needs and the budget he would have, half the total CREEP budget. This meant that almost $8 million would be at Dailey's disposal to produce Nixon's ad campaign. It was a major coup for Dailey, a handsome ex-account executive, and his young agency.

He immediately sat down with his accountant and lawyer. This was Dailey's first venture into the political world and he wanted to make sure he saw to everything. They warned him it would be imperative to separate his own company from the company he would set up to run the president's campaign. "You've got to incorporate it, and you've got to have an audit to protect your own company."

Armed with his newly acquired knowledge, he requested another meeting with Stans, the finance chairman of the campaign, and gave him a budget. In the budget was $15,000 for an audit by Price Waterhouse. "I'm talking to Maurice Stans," Dailey recalls. He pauses and remembers, in retrospect not quite believing what ultimately transpired. He gazes briefly out the window of his plush apartment on the twenty-sixth floor of United Nations Plaza. His manner is relaxed, gracious, and comfortable. He collects his thoughts and continues, stressing the respected character of his client. "Stans is a very successful businessman, a former Secretary of Commerce, former director of the Office of Management and Budget, and now he's treasurer of the campaign—a very distinguished gentleman."

"What's this $15,000 for an audit?" Dailey recalls Stans asking as he surveyed the budget.

"Well, my advisers think we should have it," Dailey replied cautiously.

"Hell, no political campaigns get audited. That's just a wasted expense. You don't need that," barked Stans.

Something told Dailey to hold fast. Dailey, his forward style tempered by his charm, pressed again. Stans didn't understand Dailey's problem. Just when Dailey was about to fold because Stans made the audit seem unimportant, something told him to raise the issue again. "In spite of the points you make, I still feel the audit's something we have to have, just to protect the company."

Stans gave in. "Well, if you really think it's necessary, okay."

This was in 1970. Campaign ethics had yet to become a major issue. Anything was okay in the eyes of the president's campaign committee as long as the objective—the reelection of the president—was met. The integrity of the players was supposedly standard enough. There were no problems to worry about; this was the incumbent president after all. Fifteen thousand dollars for an audit was wasted money as far as the committee was concerned, but it was only fifteen grand in a budget of $8 million. If it made Dailey happy, fine.

When the Watergate scandal unfolded, everybody and his congressional committee were chasing after the CREEP money supplies. After all, the guiding principle was "follow the money."

As Dailey distinctly remembers, investigators quickly learned who handled the most money in the campaign: Dailey and his group! "So everybody descended on me, en masse." Dailey smiles to himself, the scene still fresh. "All ninety people who had come to work for us had already gone home; we'd disbanded the organization and everyone had scattered. If we had tried to re-create the books after the fact, it would have been a disaster, and God knows what would have happened to me and my company."

As the inquisition piled into Dailey's Washington office, demanding answers, and certain they would find more dirty laundry, Dailey was able to reach in his drawer and hand them an audited statement from Price Waterhouse covering the period from December 1971 to December 1972. The statement covered the entire media operation. "Holding out for that audit was pure intuition. I said, 'No, I'm going to hang tough on this. It's important, hang tough.' I had no way of knowing what would happen. It was nothing but intuition."

In light of the problems that followed for some of the other CREEP participants, Dailey's commitment to his inner process and intuitive perceptions undoubtedly saved his backside. "I'll never forget running into Joe Connor, managing director of Price Waterhouse and Dailey's auditor. This was in April 1973, right in the middle of the Watergate scandal. He said 'I'll bet you liked that audit.' I said, 'Are you kidding, Joe? It was terrific.' Then he asked 'Do you know how much that would have cost you to have that audit done if you would have come to us today and asked us to go back and start that whole process? There isn't enough money in the world.'"

■ ■ ■

Dailey believes that in making decisions it is essential for a decision maker to make commitments to do things at full speed and all the way. Dailey accomplishes this through keen mental preparation. "Whenever I'm faced with a decision, I mentally rehearse, seeing the events in the future, and then project them out." Then it's up to his sense of the situation. "Every time I go against my belly," he says placing his hand on his toned solar plexus, "I'm in trouble. I can intellectualize a decision till hell won't have it, but if my belly tells me it's the wrong thing to do, but intellectually I decide to do it, ninety percent of the time I'm in trouble."

The key for Dailey is trusting that his "inner computer search," as he calls it, will come up with the right answer. Without that dedication to maintaining the courage of one's convictions, he believes the process carries no weight.

Having emerged not only unscathed but well-heeled from the Nixon campaign, Dailey's experience in matters presidential gained him a second shot at a national campaign. It was in May 1980, just prior to the final primaries, that he came on board to run Ronald Reagan's run for the White House. Reagan still hadn't put together a media organization, and he only had a little money. Dailey was called in to organize the whole process with virtually no time for preparation.

He had to hire a complete staff. That means basically having to put together what amounts to a second advertising agency. This organization would eventually handle $16 million, twice as much as Nixon's budget, in a six-week period. This kind of advertising budget would be comparable on an annual basis to Coca-Cola's $100 million advertising investment.

Bringing the people together was just the first step. Dailey and his crew had to establish the campaign plan, create the fundamental, underlying creative premise that Reagan intended to run on, and test it—all while also putting together the complete package for the upcoming convention. The nomination at this particular time was nowhere near a lock. If the nomination were secured, commercials had to be produced. The campaign had to produce a whole media plan to go on the air by mid-September. During this period, Dailey was constantly relying on his judgment and intuition; there was simply no time for anything else.

"The one thing that struck me," Dailey said, "was that the key to Ronald Reagan being successful was to position him as the chief executive of a nation state, California, and to do nothing that would enhance what I felt were the general perceptions of the man. That he wasn't a politician, but a political figure running around, who was really an actor. Most people outside of California had no idea he was a successful governor."

Dailey began viewing some of the commercials done in the earlier primaries by another agency. They were beautifully lit and well produced. But they struck Dailey as ultimately ineffective, perhaps over-produced. He thought, "It only reinforced the fundamental feeling that many people had about Reagan. They'll watch him do this, and he's superb at it, infinitely better than Jimmy Carter, and they're going to say, 'Of course, he's an actor.' So rather than getting the message, the gestalt of the message, they're going to get the visible aspects of one of the negatives they had about the man."

The decision Dailey made was to keep the creative work simple, direct, underproduced, and understated. This became the premise for the campaign. Dailey and his staff would make sure that nothing Reagan did—and nothing surrounding him—would reinforce the negative image that people had of this actor/politician.

The commercials would focus very tightly on Reagan, emphasizing the head bob and crooked smile by letting him talk directly into the camera. This panicked many of Reagan's closest aides. The candidate had a habit of saying the wrong thing. Dailey, borrowing from his football playing years under Red Sanders at UCLA, turned that problem around with a classic misdirection play. He began the creation of Ronald Reagan, the Great Communicator. A close-up, natural approach, one that banked on Reagan's warmth and avuncular manner, was taken. What he said was not as crucial as how he was saying it. This went against all the conventional wisdom that had been established about television campaigns. But Dailey knew from his years in advertising that television was nothing if not a microscope to the inner workings of the person standing in front of the lens. Putting Reagan in tight focus without soft lighting and studio tricks showed Reagan at his best, even if it flew in the face of everything that political professionals had learned about manipulating the media.

This decision put those in the campaign who thought they knew best in a tizzy. In their judgment, here was an actor. Therefore, who could better make terrific, ultraslick commercials? The biggest and loudest objections to Dailey's unorthodox approach came from the president's wife, Nancy. Her whole background in motion pictures dictated that Reagan was a star. A star must receive treatment according to that standing. He must know where his light is, where he is speaking, and how to hit his mark.

Dailey ran headlong into the fury of Nancy Reagan. Their arguments were clearly drastically opposed. She insisted that Reagan be produced to the best of every dime spent, and Dailey directed the campaign along the lines he knew to be right. As Dailey put it, he and Nancy "went right to the mat." Still, he never did convince her. He just went around her objections and did what he knew would work.

"It was a very decisive campaign," Dailey recalls, "because we ran few commercials. We kept them simple, and we repeated them constantly. All the campaign research showed that we were right on."

When the campaign began, 40 percent of the people in the United States said they didn't know enough about Ronald Reagan to vote for him. Four weeks into the campaign that statistic was 20 percent. According to Dailey, there was no time to make decisions based on long hard analysis. "These were intuitive decisions. We had to make judgments and make the commercials, commit all the funds, and then stick with them." At one point the criticism of Dailey's direction was so great that his people nearly had to bar the door to the studio in order to complete the commercials and keep certain interested parties out. The pressure drove Dailey to go to campaign director William Casey and propose, "Bill, I know I'm right, but if it's a problem for you, I'll leave."

Casey, under the tremendous pressure of being campaign director, just shook his head. "Nope," he said. "If you're right, Pete, you stick with it."

Reagan had already gone along with the idea, so Dailey just rammed the campaign on through. "I didn't ask. We just did it. Then by the time we got to the first of October and the commercials were on the air, people began to come to grips with it. It was as much making a decision as sticking with it. We made it intuitively to begin with, and then intuition said, 'Goddam it, stay with it, you're right!'"

What Pete Dailey did in both cases was to make the leap of commitment. In spite of limited time and the well-meaning cries of those who wanted to play it safe, Dailey went ahead full speed, committed to an inner feel he knew was right—and which proved to be right.

It was this ability to make the tough, high-pressure decision that sufficiently impressed Reagan to seek Dailey's aid on a matter of international concern. Reagan had already appointed him ambassador to Ireland. Then, when the administration wanted to sway Europe to put in the Pershing 2 missiles, Reagan sent special envoy Dailey to launch a propaganda campaign to redirect public sentiment. Like a modern day Alexander, Dailey's campaign won over nation after nation, much to the chagrin of the Soviet establishment.

It is notable that when the Reagan administration began to actively persuade the NATO nations of the importance of the Pershing 2's, Reagan didn't send a diplomat. He sent an advertising man. This came during a period when the Americans and the former Soviets were again bogged down in negotiations over strategic weapons.

The president sent a personal emissary to convince the NATO nations in a fashion he already knew worked because he had used it on the American public. He sent Pete Dailey to handle the problem.

Dailey's perspective of the Soviets is a fascinating one. "The Soviets," he says, "were very clever. They did an incredible job of selling their views and opinions, manipulating societies from a political standpoint, where they had no ability to do that from a commercial standpoint. It has always been a fascination of mine that a nation that was founded on not being able to sell anything—the concept of salesmanship and marketing was nonexistent—was probably the most skillful salesman of its ideas and philosophies outside of its own country. And the United States, the greatest nation in the world in terms of being able to create markets and take marketing ideas forward, was absolutely inept when it came to taking the concept of America and democracy abroad."

It was that message that the Reagan administration wanted Dailey to sell. He traveled to Geneva, where he attended the negotiations with the former Soviets. He saw the Soviets sitting at the table while the Americans made their proposals. As Dailey remembers, "The Americans were saying, 'Here's the deal, guys. You take your SS 20's that you've been putting in one every week and get rid of them all, and if you do that, we won't put our Pershings and our cruise missiles in this October.' The Soviets were literally laughing at us.

"'Come on,' they said, 'you're kidding! You're not going to be able to put those things in. Look what's going on in Germany. Look at the public opinion polls: Sixty percent of the German people are against the Pershing missile. You're asking us to give up something in exchange for something you can't do. That's crazy!'

"They were sitting with their arms folded," Dailey said brushing his forehead with his hand and checking the wave on his well-groomed, dark-brown hair. "So, I was asked to go in and see if I couldn't reshape European attitudes about this."

Dailey had arrived in the second week of January. Three weeks later Vice President Bush was due to arrive for a planned trip through England, Germany, and France. "It became patently apparent to me," said Dailey, "that if we were going to have any impact in Europe with this idea, we would never have an opportunity like the vice president's visit, which was coming up in a few weeks. Whatever we decide to do, we had to grasp it now, and get the vice president to be the lead horse on it. If he agreed to put together a strategy and be the most visible aspect of that strategy, then we can follow it up as we went along."

What Dailey sensed was that the Americans had a problem addressing international issues. "A speech would be delivered on an issue, and then we'd walk away from it. The assumption was that because a comment was made, the whole world heard it, understood it enough to be either in agreement or disagreement, and then it was time to move along to the next thing on the agenda." Dailey wanted Vice President Bush to follow a different pattern. He wanted him to deliver the message that President Reagan proposed to eliminate an entire category of nuclear weapons from the face of the earth. Dailey wanted Bush to repeat that message over and over again, wherever he spoke.

The plan was for Bush to eliminate all abbreviations and acronyms. The operation had come to be called the "Zero-Option" proposal, and nobody knew what that meant. Bush made only one simple, direct speech—and he made it again and again. "It had a great impact on Europe. You could see the change rather dramatically in the public opinion polls." By October, the European governments had enough confidence in the trend of public opinion that they didn't feel threatened by following through on the decision. The Germans put in Pershings; the British, the cruise missiles. "It was a very successful effort done in virtually no time."

Dailey's success in turning the public tide in Europe and the subsequent deployment of the American nuclear weapons had a profound effect on the Geneva negotiations. The Soviet delegation walked out. The administration's view was that NATO's position of negotiating from strength rather than weakness undermined the Soviet strategy.

The basis for this historic counterplay was a series of high-pressure strategic decisions that Dailey reached. He started with his deep knowledge of what affects people's inner thought process. If he were unable to read his own inner thoughts or trust his own intuitions, the deployment could not have proceeded. As time has shown, Dailey's ability to maneuver opinion was in the best interest of world peace. Within a few years, the U.S. and the USSR signed the INF Treaty, effectively eliminating intermediate nuclear weapons.

It has been Dailey's experience and ease in working with his intuition that has enabled him to make the strong decisions and produce the effects he has desired. The election of two presidents and the reshaping of Europe speak highly of the power of Dailey's intuition.

IRA GLASSER

THE FREEDOM TO DECIDE

Fortune favors the prepared mind, making it ripe for discovery.

LOUIS PASTEUR

IRA GLASSER HAS been executive director of the American Civil Liberties Union since 1978. Now in his early fifties, Glasser is an articulate, quick-witted, fast-talking, demonstrative man. His sense of what is important runs the gambit from protecting the rights guaranteed all Americans by the First Amendment to the all-American pastime of baseball. His large, unpretentious wood-paneled office on New York's West Forty-third Street is sparsely filled with cracked leather furniture that has been around for many years. There is "presence" in the room. A few framed pictures line the walls. One prominently displayed photograph shows the 1955 Dodgers. And like an aggressive ballplayer eager to take his swings, Glasser is not one to bail out when the game is on the line. He steps into every pitch.

Like the ability to hit a curve ball, Glasser feels the formation of a decision maker's process begins early on in the process. "I rarely wake up in the morning and say, 'This is it.' Decisions aren't that solitary. You are inevitably part of a whole orchestral arrangement of people, pressures, ideas, and perceptions. You're also a product of your past experience, which may have led you in directions that you might normally have never pursued."

As an example, Glasser spent the majority of his youthful summers working in a summer camp for the adult blind and deaf. He learned the manual alphabet and became very involved in working with the disabled. It was never his intention to become so involved. When Glasser was 16 a cousin of his, who was a social worker at the camp, got him a job. It was the summer of 1954, and Glasser waited tables for $100. He returned to that camp every summer for the next ten years, working in almost every job available.

"It had a tremendous impact on me," he says. "I learned a lot about the way blind and deaf people were treated. They were part of a ghetto that was so effectively ghettoized that it was invisible." Some of these places designed for deaf and sightless people would have ramps and no stairs. The dining rooms and walls were never brightly colored because the blind couldn't see them. They knew their surroundings were colorless because other people would tell them. They would be served food that didn't need to be cut with a knife and fork. Counselors would take the blind rowing in a boat, but they would never teach the blind how to row by making notches in the oars so that they could tell whether it was vertical or not. They wouldn't sell them beer. They infantilized these people. They treated them like they were twelve years old.

"You walk into a restaurant with a blind person," Glasser says, "and the waitress asks you what you want, and then she asks you what the blind person wants. I began to get very sensitized to the way that society treats people who are different from them. I could have told you that when I was sixteen, seventeen, and eighteen, but I didn't realize how much it would stick with me. I also learned something that I later came to understand about the way in which institutions designed to serve people really kept them dependent and infantilized, keeping them from being normal despite their disability."

Just as Glasser never intended to spend his summers with the disabled, he also never set out to become executive director of the most important constitutional rights protection organization in the land. "I didn't know what I wanted to do, I just knew I wasn't going to be a doctor or a lawyer. It was because the kids who wanted to become doctors and lawyers were the ones who wanted to become rich and nothing more. I never had anything against money, but in those years, people weren't going to law school to do justice or defend people's rights. They were going to make money. I was always interested in people and fairness. The kinds of things that might lead one to become a writer, sociologist, or even a psychologist. Those were the things that interested me."

Instead, Glasser became a mathematician. "I was good in math, but I was much more interested in history and comparative literature. When I saw myself doing something, I saw myself writing, not being a Galileo or Einstein."

After Sputnik, the opportunities for people in math were incredible. Glasser enrolled at Queens College to study mathematics. Unlike his colleagues, Glasser took the minimum number of math courses required for the major. "My last year, when all my friends were taking five math courses, I was taking one. All the rest of my classes were in history and literature. I just loved it, but the real world didn't." Glasser graduated magna cum laude in 1959. He also received an honors in literature and art and made Phi Beta Kappa.

Graduation was when the reality of his limited education really struck home. "I felt like an athlete," he says, "who was exercising one finger and had the strongest finger in the world. The rest of me was all atrophied." Nonetheless, he got his master's degree at Ohio State University in math. Rather than pursuing a doctorate in sociology and philosophy, he returned to Queens College to teach math. "It was as if the problems that I was most interested in," Glasser recalls, "were always falling in the gaps between all of those neat academic, departmental lines." It was a decade away before colleges began accepting the notion of a cross-disciplinary education.

However, to his surprise, Glasser discovered he loved teaching. He particularly enjoyed teaching undergraduates who weren't sure why they were taking math. He felt he was better with these kids, because most math teachers were people who were so naturally good at mathematics all of their lives, that they couldn't understand how someone might have problems. Glasser points out, "The classic way in which most people taught math was that they would say something. The student would give a blank look, and the teacher would say the same thing louder and then be puzzled when the student still didn't understand, as if somehow there was a hearing problem."

It was Glasser's mathematics experience that was honing his perception for the world ahead of him. "I loved making things clear to people, and explaining things I had always wanted explained to me."

In 1964, however, Glasser was caught by the political bug. This was the time of the free speech movement at Berkeley and of the civil rights demonstrations. It was also the time Glasser discovered the world of small magazines. There were more than four thousand of them at the time. If he could have, he would have subscribed to all of them. He couldn't read enough about the civil rights movement. "It was then, and remains today, the central moral issue in my life," he says. This realization made it impossible for him to simply teach math.

He wrote away to a dozen small magazines for a job, telling them he was very good and that they'd be sorry if they didn't interview him. One responded—a magazine called *Currents*. It was created by people who had foreseen the information explosion. Their idea was to take the more than four thousand little magazines that had proliferated, as well as the umpteen newspapers and books dealing with social and political issues, and excerpt the newest ideas these publications were putting forward. Glasser was hired as associate editor.

He had discovered what he thought was the best of both worlds. "I was teaching math two days a week, and I was editing this magazine. My job there was for two weeks a month to read everything I wanted on the issues I cared about. The other two weeks were to edit the magazine. I was in charge of a section on race relations that might have contained something from a war journal, a journal of sociology, a foundation report, or a speech. It was interdisciplinary and exhilarating. I became the most miscellaneously well-informed person in New York."

Eventually Glasser moved up to editor of *Currents*. Then the University of Illinois offered him a teaching appointment. He had to make a choice between the magazine and math. The magazine won. "There was no choice," Glasser said. He knew what was right for him. The agonizing over being a literary person masquerading as a mathematician was over.

It was not too much longer before one of the other associate editors on the magazine, who had been let go because of lack of funds, found a job with the American Civil Liberties Union. Glasser was only vaguely aware of the ACLU. Within a few years, his friend had become the director of the New York chapter.

During that time, Glasser started to get antsy at the magazine. *Currents* was perennially and perpetually small, and the job was becoming less fulfilling for him. "It was like doing something good in a closet," he says. "It wasn't that the work was irrelevant, but its effect was." He longed to become more active in the issues that meant something to him.

Looking around him, Glasser became convinced that Robert Kennedy would be running for president, and he made a strong effort to get on his staff. Just as a meeting had been arranged for him to talk to Kennedy, his friend at the NYCLU came to him and told him he was thinking of creating the position of associate director and wanted Glasser to take the job.

"I had this impression of them being a vaguely liberal legal organization, whose interests were narrower than mine. Again, it was also this thing I had about lawyers."

Finally, Glasser's meeting with Robert Kennedy was arranged. He told Glasser he wasn't close to running yet and was not in a position to expand his staff, but he wanted to keep in touch. Then he said something to Glasser that changed Glasser's life. It was something that he wouldn't realize was true for many years. Kennedy told him to take the NYCLU job and that he was wrong about the narrow scope of the work. "It'll get you into all the issues you are interested in," Kennedy said. "The ACLU is a very unique organization in American life. There's nothing else like it, because it operates on a radical set of assumptions (not radical in the sense of being left, but in its root sense) about what the country is based on. And it operates in the mainstream, without being a political organization. It'll get you into all the right issues."

Glasser took the NYCLU job, even though he wasn't convinced by what Kennedy had said. "I still wasn't comfortable with all the lawyers." What changed? He'd spoken with some friends of his, friends he used to play baseball with as a kid growing up in Brooklyn. And he eventually realized that the only constant in his life had been his staying true to this internal vision he had always carried with him. It was a source he could neither define nor completely focus, but it was a sense of what he wanted to be and what he didn't want to be. "There are so many variables that you have no control over," he says. "My friend gets fired four weeks after coming to the ACLU, Kennedy says yes to me, or I never meet Kennedy. The only constant is this instinct, this intuition. You have no way in the world of predicting what the culmination of that is going to be. But when I came to the ACLU, almost from the beginning, I was plunged into things that fulfilled what it was that I was looking for to the maximum extent."

Within three weeks, Glasser was sent down to South Carolina to assist in the defense of Howard Levy, an army doctor from Brooklyn who was being court-martialed for refusing to treat Green Berets—one of the earliest antiwar protests that happened inside the army. "It was as real as all the rest behind me was not real," Glasser recalls. "I was right in the middle of everything, war crimes, free speech, crimes of the military."

The army was saying that the Bill of Rights didn't apply to the military. Glasser admits until that time he hadn't given the idea much thought, but he didn't agree with the military's view. This wasn't a soldier who was out in Vietnam having to take orders. This was a guy sitting around in South Carolina talking about the war. He wasn't demonstrating. He wasn't leafletting. The story Glasser discovered when he arrived was that the doctor was being court-martialed because he used his off duty time to work with blacks on voter registration. The southern white officers didn't like a northern Yankee doing that kind of stuff.

"I came home from that rather stunned by those [Bill of Rights] arguments," he said. When he came home, he started getting calls from kids in schools who were being suspended for protesting the war or for having long hair. "I would call up the principal," Glasser remembers, "and I would hear with eerie precision the exact same thing that the army commander said about how the Bill of Rights didn't apply to the schools. He told me, 'We're just trying to run our institution. We have to have complete authority.'"

Glasser would go to these high school suspension hearings, which would resemble a court-martial. But instead of a tribunal, the principal was the prosecutor, the jury, and the judge. The decision was ordained. "It was the appearance of fairness without any procedural fairness," says Glasser. "I began to compare the school and the military and stated publicly that they were the only two public institutions in America which claimed that the Bill of Rights didn't apply to them. They were run as if they were totalitarian institutions even though one was in existence to protect free speech and the other to teach it."

They were not the only such institutions. Mental hospitals, prisons, and foster-care programs all ignored the constitution. "They were isomorphic images of each other," he said. "The arguments that the state psychiatrist, the school principal, the military commander, and the prison warden all took was the position that the Bill of Rights didn't apply to them. People would say to me, that's not the business of the ACLU. It's not traditional. It is traditional. All the rights we're protecting are traditional. What's untraditional are the settings. We're extending traditional rights to untraditional places."

Glasser takes the responsibility for pushing the ACLU into those areas. The NYCLU was the first in the country to have a lawyer working full time for mental patients' rights, student rights, prisoners' rights, and the rights of those in foster care."

Glasser was thrust into the limelight, working with all the key players in American politics. He also kept in touch with Bobby Kennedy's people once Kennedy began his White House run.

Then, waking up on June 7, 1968, Glasser heard the news of Kennedy's assassination on a Syracuse radio station. He thought it was some sort of dream, that he was reliving the JFK assassination again. For Glasser, that assassination killed a lot of things, one of which was his innocence. Two months earlier Martin Luther King, Jr. had been killed; Malcolm X was shot a few months later. "Suddenly all these people who had been the focus of the reality around whom all this seemed to swirl were gone," Glasser recalls, his distinct Brooklyn accent almost a whisper. "You began to sense that this wasn't going to be a life where you worked for someone else. If the things that you cared about were going to get done, you were going to have to do them. Even if you weren't ready, you were going to have to do it without picking your spot, you were going to have to do it from exactly where you were. I didn't think about what I was going to do, I just knew I was sort of left on my own."

Returning to the ACLU, Glasser almost immediately found himself elevated to the directorship of the NYCLU. Shortly thereafter, Glasser began to think of the ACLU as an end in itself. Robert Kennedy's words started to ring true. He saw something he'd never learned in school. To protect free speech and racial equality, it is critical in our system of government to have a force outside of government that presses those values. As Glasser explains, "Because those values are always swimming against the majoritarian tide. No matter how good a president, governor, mayor, cop, or head of school, you always end up fighting with them because they have a different set of political pressures, which could not adequately protect these values." Glasser articulated this realization in 1970, at the height of Nixon's first term, when he felt there was no hope of protecting his ideals from the inside but real hope of protecting them from the outside. "Being the organization that really nurtured all of the protest movements, making it possible for them to function, was a very exciting political place to be. It might not have happened ten years before or ten years later."

Eight years later Glasser became the executive director of the ACLU. And as he looks back over the decade and a half he has been at the national helm of his organization, he can see how all the experiences rising from a sixteen-year-old working in a summer camp for the deaf and blind have built a foundation for his decision making.

"What we call intuition," he says, "is all the experience and facts we've absorbed throughout our lives. There were many instances during this period when we didn't have all the arguments. We drove ahead, because it was the right thing to do, and discovered ten years later it was." But Glasser is quick to point out that in an organization like his, it's crucial that intuition start the process, "but then we rigorously flesh out the consequences and the arguments. If those arguments prevail in this instance, are they going to have the opposite impact somewhere else? We're in the business of trying to create legal principles out of particular cases that are going to be applied to one hundred other cases. Before we go ahead and do it, we have to figure out if we're going to be hoisted on our own petard. This is one of the things that makes us humble, that there are always unintended effects for every piece of good we do."

Glasser saw this happen in the mental hospitals. "We were right," he says, "in the area of mental patients. We blew out a lot of the unthinking closeting and warehousing of people. One of the results was that society was finally forced to release these people, but they were not required to help them. It would only help them on their terms, which was to incarcerate them. So now these people who were let out are running around on the street. It's not like these people were normal, they weren't. They needed help, but they weren't about to get it. So, now we have an increasing problem with the homeless."

New York's answer was that when the weather dropped below six degrees, the homeless would be taken to shelters—even against their will. The ACLU took the position that the city could not hold people against their will. The mayor accused the ACLU of demanding the right to freeze. As Glasser explained it, "What normal people are incapable of figuring out is what it's like to live on the street when it's five degrees and know that the shelter is worse. We have to be careful, because it's not acceptable to have them on the streets when it's five degrees.

"One of the unintended effects of our reform was that we were able to stop the government from implementing its crudest and most brutal kind of incarceration, the 'get them out of sight and out of mind' impulse, but we were unable to confer an obligation to provide care and help on the needy people's terms."

Glasser confronted a similar issue when it came to the government's decision to pick up runaway kids for their own good and put them in state training schools. As Glasser recalled, "kids were in solitary confinement, kept without food, beaten, and raped. We emptied those institutions because we were against confining kids like that when they hadn't committed a crime just because their parents were screwed up. These were kids who were neglected by their parents, and if the state had been their parents, they'd have been cited for neglect, too."

In one case, a fourteen-year-old runaway girl from Minnesota was picked up in Times Square for prostitution. The government put her into a training school. The ACLU asked why she ran away. "You think [runaways] don't know it's bad out there? You think they like being in Times Square? It's just that it's better than what they ran away from, which is incest, and what you're giving them [training schools]. I'm for supporting their free will, but that has consequences. One is that you don't solve the problem. You may prevent one problem, but then you have all these people who are out there who are not being helped, because society will not help people except on its own brutal terms."

▪ ▪ ▪

As with Robert Pittman, the conventional wisdom often pushes a decision maker outside the known, where new ideas and new ways of perceiving situations must be allowed to flourish. For Glasser, we return to the conventional wisdom because we become less flexible. "We tend to process information in terms of what's come before. By doing that, we lose the value of our intuition because we lose the ability to moderate or alter our decisions. I know all the reasons why things won't work. But I remember [that] when I was twenty-nine everyone in the organization thought that everything I thought was crazy. They'd never done it that way. I've begun to realize that the dominant reason why an organization acts the way it does is because that's the way they've always done things."

"We've never done it that way before," is one of the major reasons for stagnation in any organization. It goes hand in hand with such things as: "We're not ready for that"; "We tried that once"; and "It just won't work here." This way of thinking cannot possibly provide any forward direction for an organization. Maintaining the conventional wisdom completely stifles intuition and its by-products: creativity and innovation. Trying to do business in this world without these elements is like trying to construct a skyscraper without regard to design. You will simply never attain the lofty heights you've envisioned.

"The people I trust and rely on most," Glasser says, "think intuitively. People who analyze everything exclusively by trying to repress or ignore intuition on the grounds that it's not logical, I think, are leaving out a lot of information they don't even know they have. They think they are being rational. I think they're being irrational, because they are not rationally considering that there's information they can tap into."

Glasser believes this is something people should take into account, especially when hiring new people. "One of the things I value in people is street smarts," he says. A letter arrived on Glasser's desk one day from a very special young lawyer looking for a job at the ACLU. This man had been first in his high school class in Ann Arbor, and Phi Beta Kappa and summa cum laude at

Harvard. He went on to Harvard Law School, where he served on the law review and traveled to England's Oxford University. There he received honors in literature and history. He then returned to the United States and clerked for a Supreme Court justice. At the time Glasser received the letter, the lawyer was thirty years old and an assistant counsel to Senator Edward Kennedy's senate sub-committee.

Glasser recalls speaking with him on the phone. "I told him, 'I have all your stuff, and it's pretty impressive, but I only have one question.' He didn't seem surprised by that, because who could ask a guy like that questions, right? And he said 'Yes?' And I asked him, 'Do you have a jump shot?' He said 'What?' I knew I had him. So I said, 'I mean can you hit, can you throw, stuff like that?' And he started stammering, probably for the first time since third grade. He said, 'Well, I've played a little ice hockey in school.' I said, 'Ice hockey? You know, I knew there was trouble when I saw you were from Ann Arbor.'

"Now, he's really scattered. He said he wanted to be 'up front' with me. So I know something deceptive is coming. He said that he hadn't passed the New York Bar exam. I said to him, 'Well, I don't care about that. There's not much that a résumé like this tells me except that you can pass a test.' He asked me if he could come up for an interview. This was the coup de grâce. I said, 'We don't have interviews. We have tryouts. I tell you what, why don't you come up from Washington. There's a school yard at Twenty-sixth between Eighth and Ninth avenues. Every Saturday morning we're all there. We shoot a few hoops, we talk the First Amendment, see how you use your elbows.'"

The young lawyer never showed. "One of the things I was looking for in that exchange was how was this guy on his feet. I knew he was smart, probably one of the smartest people around. But it's like gunfighters, there's always one just a little faster. I can tell a lot by playing basketball with someone, how they come from behind, how they deal with adversity, what happens when your shot is off, how inventive they are, what happens when you push them around. Do they fight back, do they melt away? A person's character comes out if you tune into it. You don't measure people just by what's explicit."

But how does a decision maker prepare for the unexpected? How does someone ready themselves for a question about their jump shot when they're expecting a constitutional imperative? Glasser believes the answer is to avoid being rigidly committed to any fixed scenario. He should know. During the 1988 presidential campaign, he and the ACLU experienced a full frontal assault by George Bush.

Once the astonishment at being attacked by a major presidential candidate washed off, Glasser and his crew took the high elbow and pushed back. "The key instinct at the time," Glasser recalls, "was to fight back against a bigger and more powerful bully as vigorously as we could. We would use the attack as an opportunity to respond and to articulate our own vision of patriotism." Had Governor Dukakis made a similar choice, things might have been different. Instead, Dukakis didn't fight back, and he steadily lost ground in the campaign. In contrast, the ACLU's ranks grew by over fifty thousand new members.

"[Fighting back] was an instinct learned on the streets of Brooklyn," Glasser says. "What it taught us was that we need to contest with the American people for the right to represent traditional American values, and indeed, for what the phrase 'traditional American values' actually means. We have not ceded the proprietary rights to American traditions, its symbols, or the appeal of patriotism to the extremist. Rather, we invoked our eighteenth-century beginnings to define traditional American values and patriotism in a way that placed us at their center and our opponents at the margins." Glasser's intuitive response to this attack proved very successful, both in increased membership and the reputation of the ACLU. The ACLU was not an issue in the 1992 campaign.

The key to preparing for the unexpected was to do so without a ready-made scenario. "The best approach," Glasser suggests, "is to know more about your subject than anyone else and then not go in with a rigid set of expectations about what is going to happen." In this regard, Glasser is doing nothing else in these high-pressure moments than allowing himself to know exactly what he knows. As he says, "It would be a mistake to get too mystical or romantic about it, to pretend that intuition and reason occupy different spheres, when in fact they are just different stages of the same process. The flash of intuition raises the possibility, but the idea must then be tested.

"The assumption that all that information in there is good information is wrong. A lot of it is bad information. In the language of the computer people, 'garbage in, garbage out.' I think intuition gets a bad name because so much of it is based on bad information. Those kids who were cultured in the South in the thirties and forties were gonna be racist by intuition no matter what their thought processes told them. So there's some reason to be wary of intuition, but I think to deny its usefulness for those reasons is really a case of throwing the baby out with the bathwater."

So where do decisions come from? From playing baseball in the streets, from high school summer jobs, from reading, from learning what you think you'll never need, from interacting with people and life. Glasser never ran from a problem he couldn't solve. As long as he remained true to his perception of the world, he knew an answer would come. It might need to be restructured once it arrived, but he knew the answer would be there.

For twenty-five years, Ira Glasser has fought for the rights of the individual within the power of the collective. People may disagree with his values, but many of his decisions have benefited the majority. Sometimes, as he points out, "You have to stick to your principles even when it goes against the weight of opinion." That's often a difficult position to take, whether it's on the basketball court, in the halls of a mental ward, or protecting the free speech of a protestor.

R. E. McMASTER

NOW IS THE TIME

If you keep your head when all about you are losing theirs,
maybe you haven't heard the news.

ADAM SMITH, *THE MONEY GAME*

WHEN JACK BOUGHT the magic beans and went on to fame and
glory, the guy who sold Jack those beans was all but forgotten.
Well he's been found. He's been hiding out in Marble Falls, Texas,
by way of Whitefish, Montana, and Okum, Texas, and he's going
by the name R. E. McMaster. He's still got access to plenty of
magic beans, soy beans to be exact. But boy can those beans pay
off in the future for the right Jack—especially if he's got an impeccable intuitive sense of timing.

R. E. McMaster is a forty-five-year-old commodities wonder.
Clean-cut, clad in a three piece suit, his blond hair parted just
to the right of center, with a close-cropped red beard and mus-
tache rounding his face, McMaster looks at ease. It's a strange feeling to have around a commodities expert. Because of the high-
pace, quick-win/quick-lose world in which he deals, one would
expect fingernails bitten below the quick, a slightly deranged gaze,

and nervous twitching. This is not R. E., as his friends call him.

For the uninitiated, commodities are the backbone of America's heartland. They were established as a protection and a hedge for farmers against the rise and fall of their products' prices. The Chicago Board of Trade, the Chicago Mercantile Exchange, and the Commodity Exchange, New York (COMEX) are the main outlets where a person can buy futures (the projected future price of a particular commodity), in everything from gold to pork bellies to greenbacks to yen.

Fortunes are often made and lost in the commodities market as fast as you can say "soy bean meal." As in the stock market, the idea of the commodities game is to predict which way the price of a commodity will go. The problem is that the market is a lot more volatile and there is a lot more "selling short," or selling now at a higher price than the commodity in question will command at a future date, when the trader buys the quantity necessary to meet the obligation he or she entered earlier. The key to this complicated scheme is timing. And when it comes to knowing the right time to act, R. E. McMaster has proved to be a whiz.

"There are only three ways to trade the market successfully," McMaster says in his international weekly newsletter, *The Reaper*. "(1) We can trade with the trend, whether up or down; (2) We can use a trend reversal system; (3) We can buy lows and sell highs in a trading range."

Though this particular bit of information is no secret, McMaster's approach and style in utilizing this information has made him a bit of a rogue in the commodities world. This is due in part to the fact that he ties this philosophy directly to his decision making. "It takes intuition and judgment," McMaster says, "to discern which trend is correct. You have to decide whether you are in a continuation of a trend, in which case you want to make a decision that you're gonna pull back, or if you're in a trend reversal, then you want to buy bottoms or sell tops."

How does he know? "It intuitively feels right. It's as natural as putting one foot in front of the other walking down the hall."

These trends give people like McMaster a historical perspective of an era. They offer a context in which the behavior of markets can be examined and subsequently attacked.

It's important to make the distinction here between fads and trends. Even though they are certainly related, they are separated according to wavelength. The main difference between the two is time. Fads are basically wavelets, breaking close to shore and often. Trends are full-blown tsunamis that wash over all of society. Alvin Toffler, author of *The Third Wave*, sees us currently riding that third wave, following on the second wave, the industrial revolution.

McMaster's success in making decisions based on projecting trends has made him one of the most sought after commodities experts in the country. His $200-a-year newsletter, *The Reaper*, is mailed to investors in all fifty states and more than forty foreign countries. Cycle III, McMaster's telephone commodities hotline, costs investors $200 a month and has subscribers across the country and around the world.

How trusted and effective has McMaster been? First, he's been playing the commodities game for more than twenty years. Traders are considered veterans after stints of six months, if they last that long. Rapid burn out is the rule in the commodities business. But McMaster has prospered. The reason, he feels, is that he is not driven by money. "Money is a low-road motivator," he says. "It's only important to me in terms of freedom. Truth is the value force for me, and understanding how things interrelate."

McMaster believes that money is a by-product of doing things correctly, of taking the long-term view. He likens making money to a baseball player who loves the game and practices constantly. As a by-product of his efforts, he becomes a star and signs a multimillion dollar contract. There are a lot of people interested in catching McMaster's star and cashing in on the manufacture of his by-product.

A few years ago, McMaster decided to open a limited series of fifty managed commodity trading accounts. These accounts were opened with a minimum $30,000 investment. He drafted a release letter to potential enrollees on Tuesday, sent it out on Friday, and by Wednesday of the following week he was oversubscribed, having raised $4.5 million. He only took about one-third of the applicants and put the rest of the people on a waiting list, which is still filled to capacity. The reason McMaster had limited these accounts was that he believed this would be the only way to maintain the quality of the "fills," the orders of commodities, which would in turn produce a better price for the investors.

Investors return again and again to McMaster, because throughout the years he has maintained a batting average over .600, which is a Hall of Fame average if ever there was one. What makes McMaster so successful is his philosophy and approach. "You have to understand that I'm a futurist. I spend most of my time doing reading and analysis that relates to strategic planning." The indicators McMaster consults regarding these strategic plans are social, economic, political, religious, climatic, military, and financial trends. "When those ducks are lined up in a row," he explains, "I'll move toward a decision. What we're dealing with are the two elements of the economy. People and resources."

Over the last few years, the market has forced some changes in McMaster's decision-making process. He perceives those in the market today are involved in a "rampant escape from personal responsibility, which, coupled with the central bank intervention on behalf of the Federal Reserve, has basically led to the fund domination of the market." These trends have to be factored into McMaster's equations now as to when to get in and when to get out of the market.

Making decisions in this climate requires McMaster to tune in to what he refers to as a "multiple of harmonics." These include such things as Newtonian, Einsteinian, quantum physics, chaos, electromagnetic phenomena, intuition, and spiritual phenomena. "I operate as much on what I call the spiritual end of the spectrum as I do on the everyday 'Newtonian' physical reality spectrum. I then watch how the various levels of harmonics come together. And when they tumble into place, I know it's time to act."

This does not mean that McMaster acts only when everything

and everybody is in accord. In fact, it is just the opposite for him. "I find that some of the best decisions I make are consistently made when my work indicates I am in maximum mental incongruity with a popular opinion."

One such decision occurred in July 1992. The U.S. dollar bottomed out due to central bank intervention. It did so, McMaster believed, because it was oversold. Every indication pointed toward a dollar rally. McMaster's intuition told him that the rally wouldn't last. "My sense was we're going to see the dollar go to new lows, and it did a month later."

To McMaster's way of thinking, a decision maker must be willing to move against the flow of the crowd. That's creative innovation, and guiding him through these upstream currents are his integrated thought and perception processes—reason and intuition.

What this approach demands, according to McMaster, is that a decision maker be willing to take a chance on limited information. McMaster is basically describing the well-worn adage, "the greater the risk, the greater the reward." Attempting to create a new trend can either be an extremely courageous act or a foolhardy approach, depending on how you've prepared your intuition.

"If you're going to have high rewards," says McMaster, "you have to assume high risks, which means you'll have to act on limited information. The masses of people are not secure enough to act on limited information, so they avoid risk. They're risk averse."

According to McMaster's cycle watch, our civilization is in the middle of a "risk averse perspective." As a civilization ages, McMaster believes it loses its risk orientation and opts for security. "It begins to enfold on itself and no longer responds to the challenges it faces." He sees that view being upheld by the proliferation of mutual funds which are safer investments than the stock market. In fact, today there are more mutual funds than there are stocks listed on the New York Stock Exchange.

In all aspects of human life, we are searching for patterns that can offer greater understanding. By observing and anticipating trends and cycles, people like McMaster are hoping to cash in on those they believe to be successful. The Naisbitt Group, headed by John Naisbitt of *Megatrends* fame, uses daily newspapers as a way of establishing global trends. Naisbitt refers to this as "content analysis," which he likens to reading a box score of a baseball game. There are problems with this kind of analysis, as any baseball fan would immediately recognize. When looking at a box score, a line drive can look a lot like a dunk hit off the end of the bat. The box score tells how many hits a batter had, who struck out, and what the score was, but loses the style and subtlety of the way the game is played.

This problem may not be a factor in determining general trends, but it does point out that certain factors are being neglected. Newspapers may provide the facts, but the details need to be addressed by a people-oriented process. Naisbitt agrees that this is the position intuition plays best.

A similar media-oriented-trend forecasting method is called inferential scanning. Like content analysis, it is also a purposeful blend of intuition, fact, and conjecture. The process is being used by two consulting firms, Williams Inference Service and Inferential Focus. These firms slog through about 150 periodicals weekly, mulling over what they read, formulating their projections, and relaying them to their clients. According to Dun's *Business Week*, the clients of these firms value the process because of the connections that are made between apparently unrelated events and the inferences that are drawn from often minor or local events. The connections capture the subtlety and style of the market.

Reviewing history to intuitively infer future trends is very much a part of McMaster's process. He sees himself as part historian, part social scientist, part psychologist, part market analyst, as well as part sage and seer. His clues are the cycles of events. "Cycles, as they relate to mankind," McMaster believes, "are nothing more than human action progressions. In other words, just as a well-trained policeman knows how to disperse a mob, because mobs behave predictably, so too in the mass mind of the marketplace, there are high probability sequences of human action that can be predicted.

"I wait," McMaster continues, "for a confluence of indicators that give me a high probability of the next action taking place, and I move in line with the probabilities. We live in an environment of uncertainty because none of us can predict the future perfectly. That's what a decision is. A decision is always made with regard to the future. That means all decisions I make will be of necessity probabilistic."

What McMaster is describing is the ability to understand the factors that underlie human actions and correctly project how long it will take that sequence of human action to come to fruition. This way "You can project both the event and the time. I call that harmony between price and time analysis."

In early 1992, McMaster began picking up evidence that led him toward a major analysis of the market. This information would become what he called the first, second, and third hammers— major turning points that, he felt, would hit the market. He also concluded at the time that they would take place along with certain physical and sociological events. The approximate dates of these "hammers," coincided amazingly. First came the Los Angeles riots, the topping out of the Dow Jones, and the bottoming of gold and silver, all in April and May. Then came the June 28, 7.5 earthquake in southern California. Thirdly, the dollar bottomed out against the yen. The accuracy of these predictions was astounding.

McMaster is able to put these ideas into action in much the same way as a chess master approaches his game; with an ability to think in terms of his own strategy, while at the same time thinking of his opponent's. "It's the ability to think dialectically, to hold two opposing concepts in your mind simultaneously and understand both, weigh them, and perhaps even reconcile them. I call that 'Truth in Tension.'" If there is one idea that characterizes McMaster's philosophy, Truth in Tension or "TNT," as he calls it, is it.

As a decision maker in the business world, McMaster's sense of himself is more than just knowing how he will react to a given situation. It is being aware of an organization and of an organization's place in the market world. It also means being confident enough to operate in areas that aren't completely defined. Most people are only able to think in terms of black and white; few are comfortable in shades of gray. "Even fewer," McMaster says, "are comfortable understanding and holding both sides of an argument or a situation in dialectical tension till it resolves itself."

This sense manifests itself for McMaster in a feeling of peace and great security about what he is doing. "Often times," he says, "I'll go to bed with a problem and wake up the next morning and know. Just know. It's what I call working both ends of the spectrum."

This process of letting go to a decision, allowing it to unveil itself in its own time, and emerge without force, demands that a decision maker have a great deal of confidence in himself, knowing that the answer will follow. It means trusting and believing in one's own power of assimilation and synthesis. It also means being open and confident enough to reconnect to nature's time clock, rather than human time. This sense of timing, of knowing when the time to strike is absolutely right, has been McMaster's forte.

In an article in *Business Week* titled "When the Guru of Whitefish Speaks, Chicago Listens" McMaster was portrayed as a timing master. (The Whitefish in the title refers to a ranch McMaster owns in Whitefish, Montana.) In August of 1983, McMaster's sense of timing and his knowledge of his opponent (in this case the commodities market) were perfectly synchronized. As he recalls, "The whole world was bullish on higher soybean and corn prices. My work and my intuition said these markets were going to top out in late August."

McMaster took a trip to Chicago that August to visit the Chicago Board of Trade. He'd never visited before; all his transactions had been handled long distance. He went to Chicago because he wanted to see for himself what a market looked like when it topped out.

The mood over the table at lunch in Chicago was especially high. McMaster was dining with a dozen other traders who were all feeling their oats on the bullish grain futures. "There were all these heavyweights there around that table," McMaster remembers with an obvious glee in his voice. "They asked me why I was there. I told them I was in town to see a market topped out. You could have heard a pin drop. They thought it was incredible. This obviously would not be the top of the market. It turned out I was there one day prior to the top. That's what my work and intuition told me." He, of course, had already sold short, knowing prices were about to fall, and had advised his clients to do so as well.

Timing is an inner process. And since future time and past time are the power realms of intuition, a decision maker's sense of timing springs directly from this inner function. It is also not "nine to five," that is more the space of time. Timing, as McMaster has shown, is an ability to be in sync with the elements.

"It's a process of humility, patience, and listening. At the same time," McMaster emphasizes, "you've done your homework. It's not magic."

McMaster, a native Texan, is considered by other professional traders to be one of the best in the business. Gary D. Halbert, manager of Clayton Brokerage Company's Dallas Office, said, "R. E. beats the other forecasters three to one when it comes to predicting major and intermediate turns in the market." There is probably little wonder, then, that five copies of McMaster's newsletter, *The Reaper*, were sent each week to the White House at the request of the White House staff.

McMaster's self-assuredness is quite evident even in his choice of speech. He tends to speak in well-hewn aphorisms. For instance, if he's dealing with a market trend he's unsure of, his philosophy is, "When in doubt, stay out." "One of the greatest attributes of any decision maker," McMaster notes, "is patience. Any time that you have to force a decision and make it work, I've never seen it be a good decision, whether it has to do with a normal business decision, a personal decision, or an investment decision."

Or in terms of his own confidence, "It's what you learn after you think you know it all that makes the difference. The truth kills those who hide from it." And describing his approach to the pitfalls and anxiety in an amazingly volatile marketplace, McMaster simply states, "It's short-term pain for long-term gain."

McMaster's sense of self-assuredness is also based in great part on his intuition. Adam Smith maintains, "What is it that good managers have? It's a kind of locked-in concentration, an intuition, a feel, nothing that can be schooled. The first thing that you have to know is yourself. A man who knows himself can step outside himself and watch his own reactions like an observer."

Smith also thinks that a series of market decisions eventually adds up to a kind of personality portrait. He says, "It is, in one small way, a method for finding out who you are." But Smith hastens to add that when it comes to playing the market, "If you don't know who you are, this is an expensive place to find out."

McMaster has a very secure image of who he is, where he's going, and where he's been. As a cum laude graduate of the University of Houston, McMaster has moved around quite a bit since leaving his parents' home in Okum, Texas. He was a captain in the air force during the Vietnam war, serving as an instructor pilot for supersonic aircraft as well as a cadet instructor at the Air Force Academy in Colorado Springs. From there, it was just a short hop to working in Denver for real estate magnate Trammel Crow. Eventually, he moved his own operation up to his ranch in Whitefish, Montana. He then moved back to Corpus Christi to be closer to his south Texas home base. Today, R. E. and his wife, Linda, live outside Austin with their six children, ranging in age from five to nineteen years old.

Walking into McMaster's office a person gets a sense of his attention to detail. The office is meticulously clean. On the wall are the various trophies of his labor, three of which he is particularly proud. One is a letter from the president of Guatemala thanking him for his advice and assistance in helping the Guatemalan economy. There is a similar letter from the governor of the Cayman Islands. The third is a picture of the race horse, Seattle Slew, in which he owns a share in the breeding rights.

It is no coincidence that this horse of blinding speed has a prominent place in McMaster's office. His former business manager, Rick Medley, characterizes McMaster as "being quick at everything. He moves at lightning speed." It seems that McMaster's wit also moves at a similar pace. His puns and double entendres spin heads. His personal attributes demand from his staff a clear focus on detail. He wants them to be as precise in their work as he is.

Besides being an avid non-fiction business reader, McMaster does try to find time to spend away from the rigors of the market. His hobbies range from hunting to snow skiing to playing the piano though probably his favorite pastime is to spend a leisurely day with his herd of llamas, six of which roam about his land in Whitefish. He originally bought them for breeding purposes. Once he had them, however, he realized he had something more, something very special, indeed.

Rick Medley remarked, "Once you've been around the llamas for five minutes, you love them."

McMaster has discovered that these beasts are more than just an unusual pet. "They're the most sensitive animal I've ever come across." McMaster's voice takes on an almost reverent hush. It's this same sort of sensitivity that McMaster uses as a metaphor for his dealings and negotiations in the marketplace. "If you're sensitive, you're picking up data from your environment," he says, "even though it's not readily categorized in a culturally accepted way, such as nonverbal communication. If I don't see congruity and harmony between the nonverbal communication of an individual and his words, then I won't make a deal. It has to fit. It has to feel right." He's looking for harmony between his logic and feelings. And if the two are inharmonious, there is no deal.

One way McMaster has checked his feeling about this fit has been with his llamas. "They know exactly what makes a person tick," he says, "and they can tell when I come within thirty yards of them if I'm angry, if I'm going to capture them, if I'm going to feed them, if I'm gentle, exactly what my mood is. Often times I'll take people out there to test how my llamas respond to them as a cross-check to my own intuition." If the person doesn't pass the llama test, there's no deal.

Medley shakes his head in agreement. "I've seen him do it."

Obviously, the conventional wisdom of how a market trader, or for that matter a multimillion-dollar CEO, acts is not something that holds a lot of meaning for McMaster. "I'm far more comfortable," says McMaster, "with the avant garde and philosophers than I am with the Dallas/Dynasty type businessman." But in spite of, or maybe because of this approach, McMaster has been incredibly successful. Nonetheless, success, though welcome, is not the be all and end all for McMaster. "You see, there's a difference between being successful and being wise. My goal has always been to be wise. That keeps you well-rounded and balanced."

His perspective is that a person is not successful unless they are well-rounded because, "We all have only one resource, and that's limited time." It's in how we balance that resource that determines whether someone is successful or not. In McMaster's case, timing has always been his greatest asset.

As he says about himself, "I'm different." He certainly is. But he's also successful, which is why people listen to him. He makes dollars and sense.

EUGENE KRANZ

THE MAN AND THE MOON

Rationalists, wearing square hats,
Think, in square rooms,
Looking at the floor,
Looking at the ceiling.
They confine themselves
To right-angled triangles.
If they tried rhomboids,
Cones, waving lines, ellipses—
As, for example the ellipse of the half-moon—
Rationalists would wear sombreros

WALLACE STEVENS, "LANDSCAPES"

NASA's JOHNSON SPACE Center outside of Houston, Texas, is like a sprawling college campus. Large grassy sweeps separate its buildings. The space center was designed as a college campus just in case NASA didn't take off. Such are the contingency decisions that sometimes have to be made when dealing with the unknown.

Endless streams of tourists mill around the various buildings and exhibits, staring open-mouthed at the massive Saturn rockets that have carried America's astronauts to the moon. In a restricted area sit NASA's administration offices. Through a maze of hall-ways, the door to Gene Kranz's office opens on the right.

As Director of Mission Operations for NASA, Gene Kranz is in charge of operating every manned space flight for the United States. He is responsible for eleven major divisions at NASA, five major staff offices, and seven thousand people, which together control the overall direction and management of flight operation activities, engineering development, and operation of all mission support facilities. As Kranz put it simply, "It keeps me hopping. Fortunately, I've got an excellent staff. So, if you've got a good bunch of people to work with, and you've got an exciting job, you can do almost anything." It seems that at the Johnson Space Center, that what's been expected of Kranz since its inception.

One of the most important of his many responsibilities is the training of space flight controllers—the people manning the control consoles and deciding what course to take once a manned spacecraft blasts off the launching pad. Kranz, crew-cutted and firm-jawed, has been a member of the NASA-manned space team since before things ever got off the ground. He has filled his office with artifacts of space journeys, photos, and commendations. A gift from his daughters, a swimsuit calendar, lies open on his knickknack-cluttered desk. He is a confident man, speaking forthrightly with a decided Texas twang. Kranz has been committed for over three decades to one thing: planning and executing all the aspects of the United States manned space flights. An American hasn't gone into space without Kranz's looking after his or her well-being.

One of his primary duties has been to create the environment and culture for decision making on all NASA-manned flights. His organization is made up of top science and engineering graduates from around the country. "You can call them space freaks," Kranz says squaring his jaw, "but we basically have a very motivated organization. We train ourselves. Roughly one third of my organization is associated with training."

Kranz has devised a training program so rigorous that it takes two to three years to just get a flight operator ready to do the most fundamental aspects of the job. The majority of those aspects involve preparing an operator to make decisions with a window of opportunity of only twenty seconds while considering data from upwards of two hundred different sources.

A typical problem might be that a fuel cell goes out on a space-craft during a critical mission phase. What kind of a decision can be made? "Basically," Kranz says, "we make a series of smaller decisions that escalate up to the point where the flight director can then add up the facts coming in from a variety of angles, at which time I would then make a mission termination or a mission contin-uation decision. They're risk versus gain decisions."

The environment Kranz has established for making these deci-sions is unique. All participants are trained to think out loud. They voice the inner decision-making process so that if there is a fallacy in a train of thought, someone is going to pick up on it. Using this process, Kranz and his controllers can make decisions on life-threatening matters in a matter of only twenty seconds—decisions that are 100 percent correct. That's a pretty difficult track record to try and maintain. "It's amazing," says Kranz, rightfully proud, "that as you get properly trained in the use of time, twenty sec-onds is a lifetime. You can look at all your data, you can determine the problem, you can cross-check to make sure the data is valid, then you can talk to someone else and get their input. You can have half a dozen different conversations, you can have time to cogitate, and then finally make the determination of what action you're going to take."

This twenty seconds is actually a luxury. During the initial stages of the Gemini projects, Kranz had to train his operators to employ fifty to sixty different inputs and act on them with 100 per-cent accuracy in three seconds or less. This was just before engine ignition, and the operators had to make sure there were sufficient thrust capabilities to overcome gravity and get off the launch pad. Three seconds was all the time they had to act.

Decisions like these demand total commitment. They're deci-sions that may cost as much as $1 billion if a mission has to be ter-minated. They also demand an ability to synthesize information as instinctively as a samurai can anticipate an opponent's thrust. Kranz points to the emblem of his organization, which is crowned by four stars. "Those stars are discipline, morale, toughness, and competence," he says. "You've done the homework to bring you to that time and history where the decision process is intuitive. It's natural. It's something you almost feel you were born to do. These decisions have a major impact, we have to make them standing in front of the world, and we're ultimately responsible. Ain't nobody to hide behind. It's that straightforward."

If anyone knows about the kind of commitment necessary to make these high-pressure decisions, it's Kranz himself.

The eyes of the world were fixed on *Apollo 11*, which was about to carry three men to a rendezvous that would shatter our traditional perspective of our place in the universe, "with one small step." Gene Kranz was flight director of the *Apollo 11* lunar mission. It was a flight that carried with it ages of dreams, centuries of myth and vision. When that *Saturn V* rocket fired on pad 39A at Cape Kennedy and 363 feet of spaceship lifted into that cloud-spotted July sky, the spirits of people like Galileo, Verne, Copernicus, and Tycho Brahe trailed in the slip of that great moment. Men were making their way to walk on the moon.

In Houston, as *Columbia* jettisoned its first two stages, Kranz and his ground crew felt the pressures begin to rise. In three days the craft would reach the moon and initiate its final approach and landing.

One hundred hours after leaving Florida, the *Columbia* command module and its lunar excursion module (LEM), Eagle, undocked. "The Eagle has wings," heralded Neil Armstrong as he and Buzz Aldrin separated from the command module and prepared for their descent orbit insertion maneuver that would bring them close to the lunar surface.

But no sooner had the Eagle taken flight, than problems began to surface for Kranz. "We had a procedural oversight at the time we separated the spacecraft," Kranz recalls. "We didn't vent the tunnel that connected the two spacecraft. It was sort of like letting the cork out of a gun, as soon as you unbolt that thing, you're going to get basically a pop-gun effect."

In order to land the lunar module on the moon, it had to travel an elliptic course to the surface. The pop-gun effect pushed the Eagle out of its proper ellipse, pushing the craft considerably downrange from where it was supposed to be at the beginning of the descent. Immediately, Kranz and his ground crew went to work. The new trajectory was moving the landing site into a field of boulders. "We were half way to our limits for calling it off," said Kranz, "before we ever started.

"Right off the bat the guidance officer and I had to make a decision about where that air came from, and see whether it would continue to grow." At the same time, a communications problem suddenly cropped up. The engineers back in the plant had misdiagnosed and incorrectly analyzed the strength of the reflections that they would get off the surface of the lunar space-craft. Kranz had to "psych out why we couldn't communicate." The transmissions were ratty and broken. Clear communications were essential, especially now that they were about to perform a particular maneuver for which communication was vital.

If that wasn't sufficient concern, a third problem appeared. There was an instrument malfunction on the lunar excursion mod-ule. The crew couldn't read the values for the alternating current electrical power that drove the gyros and some of the displays. Kranz had to see to that, too, determining from the ground whether everything still looked good.

The two spacecraft were still close—Armstrong and Aldrin in the LEM and Mike Collins in the command module. They were circling the moon on their thirteenth orbit. Every time the crafts went behind the moon there was what the flight operators referred to as a LOS, or loss of signal. This, obviously, was expected. Mission Control broadcast to an entire world waiting breathlessly by televisions and radios, "We're coming up on fif-teen minutes now until LOS with the lunar module. Flight direc-tor Gene Kranz has advised his controllers to review all their data and take a good close look at the spacecraft in preparation for a go/no go decision on the descent orbit insertion, or DOI."

Kranz's decision was go. "I made the decision in light of these problems to press on, because, individually, none of them were threatening." The decision had to be made quickly because the DOI maneuver began while the craft was on the far side of the moon and out of communication with the ground. When the Eagle had reemerged and acquisition of signal from the craft was acknowledged, Kranz gave the next go—for powered descent. This despite the fact that two minutes into the powered descent all these problems continued nagging away at the flight director and his staff.

Suddenly things took a turn for the worse. An alarm sounded on the LEM, and Neil Armstrong began calling out "12 02, 12 02." Kranz was then faced with a major decision that was absolutely time critical. The computer was telling them it didn't have time to do all the jobs they had programmed it to do. It went immediately to the highest priority job, and when it ran out of time to finish the rest of that job, it went back to the top of the priority list and kept proceeding in that manner. "The concern," Kranz said, "with what we called this 'bail-out' alarm was that the computer keeps getting slower and slower and slower. This alarm then turns into the 12 02 alarm where the computer will go to halt and wait for further instructions. And when it's the computer that's bringing you down to the surface of the moon, that is not the place to have it happen."

A month before, this took place in a simulation run. The computers began flashing a 12 02, and the simulated landing had to be aborted. But according to one of the NASA controllers, Charlie Duke, after that occurrence, "Kranz had done a brilliant thing." He gathered all the people who were involved in this area: designers, controllers, and support people. They went step by step through everything that could possibly happen to cause an alarm. They even went over possibilities that no one would ever expect. One of those alarms that no one believed was ever possible was a 12 02 alarm. Nonetheless, Kranz had a notion and he wasn't about to take a chance. He prepared his crew.

The decision was made after the simulation that if the 12 02 alarms were not constant and the computer could catch up right away, they could still go for landing.

That was simulation, though. Now, in real time, Kranz and his guidance officer were faced with the decision whether to abort the first attempt to land on the moon, just minutes away, or continue. First they had to diagnose what was happening with the on board computer, then they had to work out the problem of the landing site. "We kept picking up more and more of the work load on the ground." Kranz remembers: "All the way through I was keeping track of the problems, but again I knew we were safe and that we should continue to the ground."

There was nothing to be done about the downrange error except find a new place to park the LEM. But as the craft got closer to the surface, another problem arose. A light had come on at Mission Control. The Eagle only had thirty seconds of fuel left.

The plan had originally been that the craft would be down by that point, but since the craft had experienced the separation error, the new trajectory had put them into the middle of a boulder field. They now had to maneuver around this very hazardous obstruction, and this process began eating into their fuel reserves. Kranz decided not to tell the crew at thirty seconds. But at fifteen seconds, when the craft still hadn't landed, he informed the crew, telling them they were beginning the countdown to an abort. But Kranz knew they'd get down. He gave the final go.

"When we landed on the moon," Kranz recalls, "we had seven seconds of fuel remaining."

The call went out, "The Eagle has landed." The world went crazy. People cheered in the streets. In Paris, on the Champs Élysées, the French had set up television sets in shops and elegant showrooms. This was not merely an American event, it was a human event, radically altering humanity's worldview in a completely peaceful manner.

Back at Mission Control, Kranz's job was not complete. While all the dignitaries were whooping and hollering behind a glass partition, Kranz had to move from the plateau of landing on the moon to what were called the "stay/no-stay" decisions. Once on the moon, they had to go through a countdown for a possible immediate liftoff from the moon. During that roughly sixty-second countdown, they had to take a look at the spacecraft to make sure nothing had been damaged. They had to determine that all systems were still safe. They had to ascertain that the spacecraft hadn't landed in a soft spot and was about to tip over. They also had to make sure that the plume of exhaust from the powered descent hadn't knocked any rocks into the tanks.

The sheer excitement and the emotional toll left Kranz, for once, at a loss. "I couldn't get started. I was speechless. I'd come to the point . . . " his voice trails off as he returns to that July 19 Texas afternoon. "The consoles of the TV monitors had these handles on the sides, and I was holding on so hard during that last minute, using my foot key to communicate, I couldn't start the countdown process going. I just finally hit my forearm on the console (pulling it off the handle), and seriously, I had a hemorrhage all the way from my elbow up to my wrist I'd hit it so hard. Finally, I got it unlocked and proceeded to start the countdown for the stay/no-stay decision. Again we made it, and elected to stay. It was only at that point, where we could really sit back for a few seconds and say, 'Hey, we actually landed on the moon.'"

Kranz's knowledge, his training, and his sense of limits, both of time and capability, brought him to the point "where the decisions became intuitive." Then his commitment to those decisions, and his spirit of being true to himself and to his methods paid off.

In a less political arena, there are also times when an intuitive decision is the only possible recourse in saving someone's life. As Director of Mission Operations, Gene Kranz has been called on to make a few of these decisions. One in particular began with a simple, calm communication, "Houston, I think we have a problem."

Three days earlier, *Apollo 13* had lifted off from Cape Kennedy on an early spring morning. Astronauts Jim Lovell, John Swigert, and Fred Haise had visions of becoming the third set of astronauts to go bouncing around the moon. But when they were over halfway to the moon, a problem surfaced.

The best word to describe life on board an Apollo spacecraft is "cramped." The craft for *Apollo 13* was composed of three sections: the command module, the command service module, and the lunar excursion module. The cone-shaped command module, the astronauts' home, stretched to a height of only eleven feet. Here, the three astronauts spent most of their time. This compartment rode between the service and lunar modules.

On that fateful April 13, Lovell and Haise had just finished checking out the LEM, Aquarius. Lovell was already in the tunnel back to the command module, Odyssey, where Swigert was manning the controls. Suddenly, there was a large, loud bang.

Lovell and Swigert thought that Haise had merely released a valve on the Aquarius as planned. But that was not the case. Haise returned to the Odyssey, immediately scanned the instruments, and found that a main electrical system was rapidly decaying. Then Swigert notified Mission Control. Gene Kranz was on duty at the time as flight director. Kranz and his crew immediately assessed the situation as life-threatening. The first course of action was to have the crew bail out of the command module into the lunar module, shutting down the power supply in the Odyssey. The LEM with its power supply would become the astronauts' lifeboat.

Once the crew was in the LEM, Kranz was faced with two options, both geared toward preserving the systems in the best way possible—and thus the astronauts' lives.

The first choice was to take the shortest and fastest way home. This would mean that the astronauts would have to use the service propulsion system on the damaged service module and jettison the LEM—if the service propulsion system was capable of being used.

The second choice was to take the longest way home: around the moon and back to earth. This meant the astronauts would have to rely on the LEM spacecraft, but the LEM was designed to be used for only about twenty-four hours. The dilemma for Kranz in this case was that he would have to make the spacecraft last ninety-six hours. No one knew if this could be done. Even that, however, wasn't the major consideration. The real point of contention was that once Kranz got the craft back to earth, he still would have to find some way to separate the command module from the LEM.

The choices for Kranz were then based on the unknowns of the LEM spacecraft (making it last ninety-six hours) versus the unknowns of the service propulsion systems on the service module.

"I had a gut feeling about this," says Kranz. "Because I had flown a large number of LEM missions—I used the LEM to land on the moon, and in *Apollo 5* and *9*—I knew it was a tough vehicle. My gut feeling said I had a better chance of solving that problem than risking utilizing the service propulsion system when I had no visibility into it. I just felt I had more control over the unknowns using the LEM."

Kranz reached his decision. The three astronauts would spend the next four days holed up in the tiny LEM designed for the temporary transport of two men.

"Once I got into the process (with the LEM)," Kranz says, "I figured I would find a solution. But if I used the service propulsion system and I was wrong, I would lose all my options." He would also have lost three astronauts and the spacecraft. "My intuition told me to keep my options in front of me, even though the risk was very high going either way."

As history shows, Kranz's intuition was right. The power and air supply on the LEM held out. The LEM engines powered the spacecraft around the moon and back toward earth.

Approaching Earth, the Aquarius engines were fired again. The flight engineers had been working furiously on finding the right angle into the earth's atmosphere. They would have one shot at it. They had to thread the craft through a narrow gateway out of space. Once the engines were fired, the astronauts moved quickly back into the lifeless command module, cut loose the damaged service module and their lifeboat, Aquarius. For the first time, the astronauts saw the severe damage to the service module. Had Kranz decided to take them home the short way, they would certainly have lost their lives.

As it was, they now had this one final shot. When the chutes appeared on the command module, a cheer went up at Mission Control. But not until forty-five minutes after splashdown, when the aircraft carrier *Iwo Jima* picked up the weary astronauts, did the tension Kranz had been laboring under lift.

Kranz had trusted his intuition in a situation where the most logical choice—bring them home fast—was the decision that would have killed them. Kranz called it a gut feeling. He made the decision with lives hanging in the balance, and that certainly took guts. It took trust in everything he knew and everything he had learned. It required a leap of intuition of literally astronomical proportions. Thanks to that, Lovell, Swigert, and Haise returned to tell about their three-men-in-a-tub trip around the moon.

The saying that "experience is not what happens to you, but what you make of what happens to you," would certainly pertain to Gene Kranz. From an intuitive perspective, experience provides a foundation for point of view. As Alan Kay has said, "POV is worth 80 IQ points." And when it comes to making decisions, point of view is probably the most important aspect.

How does one go about developing the proper perspective? That kind of question is almost like asking how does one go about choosing a religion. A major portion of a person's perspective has to do with values and beliefs. If a decision maker's value and belief systems are narrow, then their point of view will probably be narrow as well. If, however, a decision maker is open to as many different viewpoints as possible, then, as Kranz mentioned earlier, a tremendous amount of information can be gathered in as short a time as twenty seconds.

Intel Corporation's Andrew Grove calls this information gathering "free discussion." Another name for it is brainstorming. By any name, it is an excellent stimulator of intuition. In an atmosphere where people feel they can freely express themselves, brainstorming encourages many differing points of view. It is crucial, however, that this dialogue is conducted in as nonjudgmental a way as possible. All ideas in a brainstorming session should be recorded. Only later, after the brainstorming session, should the points be prioritized. When everyone is treated as an equal in the brainstorming process and no one's ideas are squashed, some incredibly innovative and creative problem-solving solutions can be brought forward. During these free discussion sessions, a decision maker needs to listen. As Grove points out, "each time an insight or a fact is withheld and an appropriate question is suppressed, the decision-making process is less than it might have been."

As Kranz has done at NASA, an organizational culture must be created that will sustain an environment that values various and often conflicting points of view and considers many options. The creation of this culture is the job of the leader.

The importance of this brainstorming process to the decision maker is that the better he or she has listened, the better prepared the decision maker's intuition will be. Again, point of view has to do with experience. The broader the perspective, the more decision makers can make of what happens to them.

Kranz and his flight operations training people recognize this. They have instituted a program called "Cockpit Resource Management" (CRM). This process was originally created to deal with crisis management in the cockpit. According to Kranz, "it allows both flight crews and flight operations people to sharpen their intuitive response to the people they are working with to find the solution to a problem."

CRM dynamically changes the roles and missions of the flight crew players. The traditional cockpit relationships of pilot, copilot, and engineer have been modified so that if a problem occurs, the cockpit players can brainstorm rapidly without having to fear criticizing the commander. If the preestablished procedures and techniques are not delivering the desired results and the crisis is continuing, all of the players are empowered to break out of the preconceived procedures to try to find a solution. The captain of the ship may be in charge, but he or she is no longer in absolute control.

These team building exercises are employed with flight controllers, too. Frank Hughes teaches these CRM classes for NASA. He pointed out that "the larger the group, the more difficult the process. What we try to do is get these controllers to say, 'I may feel like a salmon swimming upstream, but I think there's something wrong and what we are seeing is just the symptoms.' We want people to voice these opinions in the control center arena."

The exercises used in this training are devised to simulate failures that would purposefully lead the controllers toward the wrong conclusion. By doing so, Hughes and Kranz believe that they are teaching their people to listen to their intuition and act on it. Of equal importance is the breakdown of the traditional hierarchical relationships. Hughes believes that if more cockpit members or crew members acted on their intuitive perceptions and spoke up, fewer people would die needlessly in travel-related accidents. As Hughes said, "If the captain of the *Titanic* had a crew member on board like that, they might have done better."

For this kind of dramatic culture change to take place in the cabin of a spacecraft or in the control center of a space flight requires a tremendous trust by the leadership in the intuitive responses of those involved. Kranz knew that by establishing a receptive culture, the responses would come, just as they had time and again for him.

It is important to note that even though Kranz and his highly trained crew have learned to listen to their intuitive responses during high-pressure situations, there are times when unforeseeable events transpire. The *Challenger* disaster was one. Both at the time and in retrospect, Kranz says he can remember nothing that told him, "Hey, today probably ain't a good day to fly." His job was to observe the dimensions of the overall flight activities from liftoff through the time the crew left the spacecraft. Whether or not to launch *Challenger* was a decision handled by the mission management team and the program director at the Kennedy Space Center, not Kranz.

If experience is what you make of what happens to you, did the *Challenger* experience change Kranz on decision-making process? One thing he realized was that "For the first time in my life I had to come to grips with the fact that the American public wasn't tuned to the risks of space flight or exploration. This business we are in is risky by its nature, and we've tried very hard to articulate why we think these risks are important. We try to manage the risks, but we don't think about quitting if we had a bad day."

The loss of *Challenger* put an added burden on the twenty-sixth flight of the space shuttle. Kranz's concern was that another failure would cause an enormous delay in the space program. "For the first time in my life," he said, "I felt a pressure I was unaccustomed to. There's a lot of things we do in space that have absolutely never been done before. Some of these things aren't going to work."

One such risk took place in July 1992, when NASA tried to drag a tethered satellite on the end of a twelve-mile cable through the very thin atmosphere of space. Prior to the launch, Kranz makes clear, "It was almost impossible to predict what would happen. We're writing the textbook on physics. But we have to find some way to tell the American public we're working in an area where nobody has been before. Since *Challenger*, we have come face-to-face with this issue of risk with every flight. We know that the whole future of NASA, the United States space program, and maybe the future of the American economy rides with every damn mission we fly. To put it bluntly, it ain't smart to have that kind of a pressure on the system."

This pressure, Kranz believes, is what's keeping the space program from operating as efficiently as it could, both in terms of time and money. And keeping an eye on the time and money spent on mission operations is a big part of Kranz's job. Seeing to the details of this massive operation, and that NASA's flights continue to be almost 100 percent successful demands a clear sense of direction. For Kranz, this is a proven part of his intuitive abilities. "I pick a course," he says, "and then I get my antennas up. Once I start down that course, I look, listen, and observe to see if there's anything that seems amiss. Generally, I tend to know that within a very short period of time. And with these enormous amounts of information moving about very rapidly, I feel it in my body, yeah, we're moving the right way."

When you're in a spacecraft orbiting 250 miles above the surface of the earth, you want someone whose antennas are well tuned to all frequencies. Sometimes intuition is the only function available at the moment of a life or death decision. There is simply not enough time to follow all the procedural steps. And as the *Apollo 13* astronauts can affirm, having a tried and trusted intuitive sense can mean the difference between life and death.

DR. LEWIS R. GOLDFRANK

EMERGENCY!

I don't want to achieve immortality through my work. . . . I want to achieve it through not dying.

WOODY ALLEN, *DEATH (A PLAY)*

HAVING THE TIME to run a battery of tests in order to make a proper diagnosis, to explore and debate with colleagues the intricacies of a baffling disease, is a luxury some doctors rarely have. As chief of the emergency services department at New York City's Bellevue Hospital, Dr. Lewis Goldfrank is lucky if he has time to learn the name of his current patient. In the emergency department, Goldfrank and his doctors, nurses, students, and volunteers are continually confronted with life and death decisions that must be made while acting on extremely limited information. Often all they have to work on are the obvious symptoms, their sense perception, their experience, and the synthesis of that into intuition.

When Bellevue first opened its doors for care in the year 1658, its purpose was primarily to serve the soldiers and slaves of the

Dutch West Indies Company. At the time, New York City, then New Amsterdam, had a population of about one thousand.

Hospital care has undergone a few significant changes from the time of barber-surgeon Jacob Hendrickssen Varrenvanger, the founding father of Bellevue, but Bellevue's location hasn't changed since the early 1800s. This dowager queen of inner-city municipal hospitals, a massive brick and glass institution, still stretches along Manhattan's East River. Few American monuments share the kind of history this hospital has seen. As Page Cooper described it, Bellevue stirs images of "drama, despair, and miracles, all timed to the very heartbeat of the city." It took in yellow fever victims during the War of 1812, and takes in the indigent and mentally disturbed of today's Manhattan. Whenever another hospital doesn't want a patient, he or she ends up at Bellevue.

The emergency services department lies buried toward the backside of Bellevue. It is under the supervision of Dr. Lewis R. Goldfrank. His small overcrowded office, with its cluttered bookshelves, one of his children's watercolors on the wall, sits on the edge of his massive charge. This is not a quiet place away where Goldfrank can duck in to avoid the constant onslaught of the emergency department. Even here the atmosphere is charged. Everything and everybody feels poised and at the ready. It's a climate on which Goldfrank thrives.

The call comes in from the paramedic. They're bringing in a comatose victim. A gurney bangs through the doors and the patient is wheeled toward an emergency room. A doctor is already assessing whether the patient is alive or dead, breathing or not breathing, thinking or not thinking. Vital signs are checked: pulse, blood pressure, respiratory rate. Is the patient blue (no oxygen)? Is the patient yellow (deeply jaundiced with liver failure)? Is the patient white because he or she has no blood left? These observations start the emergency decision process. "The difference between our responsibility and elsewhere in a clinical setting is everybody else assumes their patient is alive. Our first step is to see if the person is alive or dead. Then is the patient emergent, urgent, or nonurgent?" This is the process of "triage," where a doctor must decide if the patient needs immediate attention. Does the doctor have a half hour, an hour, a half day, or a week?

Goldfrank describes the setting of the emergency department in terms of a chaotic art gallery. Most art museums are organized and arranged by rooms. But, "if you had the Rembrandts mixed with the Gauguins and Mirós," says Goldfrank, "and you had everything thrown together in total chaos, and you went from one emotion to the next, say from a *Guernica* to a field in southern France by van Gogh. . . . That's the experience in an emergency area. Totally unpredictable."

One minute a doctor is working on a wealthy accident victim, the next on a comatose street person. The emergency department faces a dayload of comatose patients. This forces the emergency doctor to be a detective. With only limited information, often no history or laboratory data, a doctor must utilize every possible shred of evidence that can be gleaned from the patient's appearance, pockets, or odor. Anything that might establish where the person has been is important. Is the patient wearing an armband because he has been in another hospital recently? Is he wearing a medical alert bracelet? Is there a scar on the vein? White powder near the nose?

As the doctor looks through the clothing, perhaps a pill bottle will be found with the name of a pharmacy. Goldfrank notes that 50 percent of all drugs claimed to be taken in drug overdoses are not the drugs taken.

One of the few clues that an emergency physician has that a doctor in another section of the hospital doesn't have is that the patient is dressed in his primary garments, i.e., his own clothes. It is a real plus for Goldfrank to be able to see how the person was dressed in the community. He can see if a hat fits properly. If not, does that mean there might be a brain tumor? The shoes don't fit; there's fecal or urinary incontinence. These are signs that Dr. Goldfrank must read in order to fit together the pieces of the pattern that landed this poor unfortunate in the emergency department.

The job is further complicated by the fact that at Bellevue, Goldfrank and his staff have to continually distinguish between the patient who is truly sick in body from those who are sick in mind. Goldfrank has one axiom that he uses at all times, "If the person looks sick, he is sick."

One of an emergency department doctor's most important tools is intuition. Goldfrank looks for a highly developed intuitive sense in the people who work for him. Intuition is what separates the doctors who are more structured, algorithmic, and have difficulty in emergency services from those who savor the unpredictable and thrive on the creativity it demands.

Goldfrank cites the case of an old woman who recently came into the emergency ward. She was complaining about pains in her chest. Goldfrank examined her. He took an electrocardiogram, or EKG, and found nothing. He checked all her vital signs—nothing. He ran through all her recent and past experiences—nothing. She just complained of chest pains. Without any evidence, and in light of the fact that he continually must separate those who are really sick from those who just think they are sick, Goldfrank immediately checked the woman into the intensive care unit. There, within a few hours, she had a massive heart attack. Had he released her back onto the street, the coronary would have killed her.

Goldfrank is constantly testing his doctors' intuitive responses. There are continual hypothetical scenario questions asked of interns and residents alike. Such as, "given this limited information, what action do you think should be taken?" Diagnosis in the emergency ward setting is often based on a doctor's ability to synthesize evidence and experience quickly. Intuition is an essential part of the process. According to Goldfrank, there just isn't the time to address all the algorithms, the lists, or to follow all the steps. "It's the doctor as a detective," Goldfrank repeats. His primary tool: "Intuitive logic."

Over three hundred people a day find their way into Goldfrank's emergency department. They wait in rows of red and blue plastic chairs, a TV pouring a constant low level hum of noise. A whole wall is covered with a brightly painted child's mural, depicting the children's views of life and death; ghosts, helicopters, a green earth being held by black and white hands, a monkey, a menorah, a yin-yang symbol. A child's life in the city.

Patients to the emergency department are met not just by doctors and nurses, but also by high school students from local schools. These are kids who might be struggling in school or maybe trying to understand the value of life, what illness is, or why people have problems. There are also college students thinking about careers in medicine and health care, volunteers known as patient advocates, and medical students. Before these aides and students ever encounter their first patient, they all receive a course in ethics. They learn to understand what brings people to the emergency department—the medicalization of social issues.

"We try to develop a system," Goldfrank says, "that forces people to discuss the human being simultaneously with the circulating toxins or electrolytes or the fracture. They've got to understand how to account for the patient. They've got to make contact."

Goldfrank accomplishes this by making sure his people take a history and talk to the person. To treat them effectively, Goldfrank's people have to understand the world that person comes from. They must know what homelessness is and what poverty, substance abuse, wife battering, and alcoholism are. "If they do that," Goldfrank says, "then they begin to feel for the person much more than what the CAT scan might show or the X-ray. That's not the person. These people come in in bad shape, and they've got to have confidence in me. They've got to believe that I can help them. I've got to show them that I'm concerned. I've got to develop some understanding of why they're here, and I've got to do it immediately." Unlike the doctor whose patient is in a bed elsewhere in the hospital, Goldfrank doesn't have the luxury of time. "I've got to solve my problem, now."

Fortunately for those people who find their way into Bellevue's emergency department, Goldfrank literally wrote the book on toxicologic emergencies. His textbook describes all the ways people react to various poisons, and what an emergency practitioner can look for and should do in almost any poisoning circumstance. For instance, what does an emergency physician diagnose when a family of four is brought into the hospital in various levels of consciousness—two in complete heart arrest and two barely conscious? What do they know when the ambulance drivers report that the family pets were found dead in the room? What are the clues to go by? What interventions does the doctor take? Or perhaps a middle-aged, noninsulin diabetic man is found unconscious in a greenhouse and rushed in a deep coma to the emergency department. There was no sign of trauma or odors. What are the major diagnostic considerations? What immediate therapeutic interventions are indicated? What substances are capable of producing this syndrome?

Goldfrank trains his people to sharpen their intuitive sense. "I always keep a notebook in my pocket and I write down the questions people ask me. I collect them and use them in lectures. Like the ten most common reasons a patient comes in with blue skin." This kind of training prepares the doctors so that when they see a problem they're checking themselves to see what bells go off in their minds.

Goldfrank returns to his detective motif. "Like Sherlock Holmes, you have to determine what the problem is. It might seem rare, but how does it relate to other issues? Nothing is irrelevant. Each piece of information is valuable, even if it isn't understood today. You ask people to look, smell, to feel, to ask for descriptions, and to accomplish the evaluation through an understanding of things that you might not understand." In short, you synthesize what you know and allow each person's intuitive logic to take over.

Smell is a particularly important sense in this process. It is also one that decision makers often associate with decisions. We've heard many decision makers make the statement that they can smell a decision. There is good reason for this. The olfactory nerve is composed of brain cells and is connected directly to the limbic system, which is that part of the brain that controls memory. It is the only sense directly connected to the brain. This explains why a person might go into a kitchen and smell a turkey baking in the oven and immediately be transported back to a childhood event associated with that smell.

The late Dr. Lewis Thomas wrote in an essay entitled "On Smell," "The act of smelling something, anything, is remarkably like the act of thinking itself. Immediately, at the very moment of perception, you can feel the mind going to work, sending the odor around from place to place, setting off complex repertoires throughout the brain, polling one center after another for signs of recognition, old memories, connections."

What, then, makes a good emergency doctor? Goldfrank rattles off the list of qualifications we can only wish all doctors might have. "Enjoys other human beings. Likes to solve unsolvable problems, has high energy, intellectual curiosity, interested in everything to do with the human body, and willing to deal with someone who's got maggots on him. Can deal with someone who's worried about losing a little bit of hair or has a rash on a hand, or someone who's got a stab to the chest. This is someone who's really the universal physician, interested in anything under any circumstances any time."

So how does Goldfrank determine if he has a Hippocrates to fill his needs? He says that as a joke he sometimes uses a three pencil illustration. The first pencil is long but has no eraser. The second pencil is short and has a full eraser. The third is used equally at both ends. From the first pencil we learn that this person is unable to take the first step in writing anything down and is always erasing. This is not someone Goldfrank wants in his department. The second person writes at breakneck speed, but never bothers to erase anything. This person has no humility and has an unwillingness to accept that he or she can be wrong. It is the person who used the third pencil equally worn at both ends, that Goldfrank is looking for.

This is the person Goldfrank believes who can "look at a problem that looks just like the same one they've seen a hundred times and say, 'did you notice that peculiar dampness of the skin?' They've got to have their eyes open for things that are important.

They've got to have the desire to work with others and know how to handle autonomy. These people need to be able to shift roles easily. They need to be able to function when the place is a mess. Can they pick up a piece of paper off the floor? If they can't adapt and be creative in solving problems, they're not going to survive here."

Goldfrank walks every new person through the midst of the department so they can see the chaos. "The person that's going to make it sees the order in the process, the potential for being able to do something, the excitement. The person who sees people milling about and no order will have a very hard time with us. With over two hundred employees addressing the needs of the critical and suspected critical, Goldfrank has to know his people are the ones who see the pattern in the chaos; the doctors who can recognize that the family admitted in various states of consciousness were exposed to carbon monoxide poisoning and that the diabetic man who had collapsed in the greenhouse was overcome by the insecticides he had been using. The symptoms can only point toward the illness. The caregiver has to be able to apply everything they've ever learned, everything they've ever seen, and then look for anything they've never seen, all the while listening to that inner process to synthesize the information they are amassing.

For Goldfrank, the catastrophe is immediate. A young woman comes into the emergency department and is standing in line, waiting to be seen. She is crying. She provides little history to the admitting nurse, but she's confused. Suddenly, she drops into a coma. A nurse comes for Goldfrank, telling him of her bizarre behavior and her crying. He immediately went to the stricken woman. She was cool and clammy. His first thought was a behavioral abnormality. Then it dawned on him. Maybe she was hypoglycemic, that is, had very low blood sugar.

Goldfrank brought her in and immediately gave her glucose. When she came back around, she gave them a history and they discovered that someone had given her some pills that had poisoned her and lowered her blood sugar.

"Crying," Goldfrank said later, "is a very atypical pattern, especially since she wasn't crying and being lucid. You had to think that something very strange was going on in the process. You have to ask, what causes crying? There are a thousand reasons that you've seen in your life. Most people who are crying when they come into the emergency department are doing so because they're lost, or their husband's been injured, or their wife's got a problem. But someone coming in crying and not being able to express themselves is very strange and very important. Everything that exists has some relevancy to us. We may have to put it on a long list, because we're not clear what it means right now, but it gives us a clue." The intuitive aspects of Goldfrank's work are about being open to the unknown, being able to recognize he's dealing with something new and important, and being able to correctly respond to the situation. Had he not trusted his intuitive abilities and recognized the hypoglycemic reaction the crying woman was having, Goldfrank would have been speaking to police officers about a homicide. Instead, the woman recovered.

Making life or death decisions is part of a doctor's job. But how does a doctor know if he or she is making the right life or death decision? The weight of such determinations is enormous.

Dr. Edwin Rutsky, director of the Medical Dialysis Facilities at the University of Alabama, Birmingham Medical Center, is one of this country's leading nephrologists (kidney specialists). He has also been acknowledged as one of the top one hundred doctors in the country. One aspect of Rutsky's overall responsibilities is deciding which kidney patients will go on dialysis, which will receive renal transplants, and which patients are terminal and therefore will receive no such specialized treatment.

Establishing whether a patient is a suitable candidate for treatment is a very tough decision. These patients for the most part are nearing what is called end-stage renal (kidney) disease. These are decisions that are difficult for the doctor as well as the patient. As Rutsky describes them, "They are emotionally very expensive decisions. They take a good deal out of me."

In forming these decisions, Rutsky must ultimately decide

what is reasonable therapy for a patient whose life has been extended beyond its natural course. Often, they are faced with extraordinary and life-threatening illnesses. "At what point do you say 'enough,' and stop and pull back?" Rutsky asks. "How do you pull back when you know that pulling back means the death of the patient?"

Medicine, as Rutsky points out, is not an exact science. Doctors make decisions based on their best judgment. Like decisions in the business world, that is predicated on experience, research, the exploration of options, and a thorough analysis of the facts. This is no time for a doctor to be acting on whim, deciding off the top of his head whether a life is salvageable or not. Decisions like this must come from the synthesis of all possible information.

Some of these decisions have recently been taken from the doctor's domain by the federal government. In the mid-1970s, Congress passed a law that provided financial support under Medicare for patients with end-stage renal disease. This enactment has given people the perception that they are entitled to chronic dialysis care or transplantation. Prior to this, positions on available dialysis units were only for those young enough and potentially productive enough, or who had a reasonable hope of rehabilitation, or who were clear-cut candidates for transplantation. Now, people who once would have been rejected as unsuitable are entitled by law to treatment.

"What Congress essentially did," says Rutsky, "was provide physicians with a blank check. The physician's first primary job is to preserve life. There are times, I think, when a physician has to decide that it is no longer justifiable or reasonable to prolong life, because the quality of life is not adequate. Now, I'm not saying you stop feeding people, [or] withhold antibiotics. I am saying that people with incurable illnesses that are about to kill them need not continue hemodialysis."

Rutsky points out that because of the federal support, these kinds of decisions to treat or not to treat a patient who is in deteriorating shape are in one sense easy: You put them on if there's a space. But they are also very difficult because, "You know that many of these people are not good candidates for dialysis. You know that somebody with congestive heart failure who has severe underlying cardiac disease as the cause of their heart failure, [or] who is blind, [or] who has had an amputation and has a black toe on the other foot, [or] who is diabetic; you know that person, if he lives a year, may have a year of utter hell in terms of quality of life. What do you do with a patient like that?

"Your better judgment says it is not reasonable to spend $28,500 of the public money to support a year of dialysis, not mentioning what it might cost for the hospitalization. The government has created the climate where if the family says, 'You have to dialyze. We want him dialyzed. We don't care what his quality of life is, we want Daddy alive.' It becomes more difficult."

Dr. Rutsky's decision to dialyze someone is always made as a pact between the physician and patient. "It is the patient's right," Rutsky says quietly, "at any time, to say, 'No more. I want off,' fully knowing that it will kill him. I don't think that's suicide. That's not like putting a gun to your head. It is the right of the patient as long as he is competent to make the decision to say 'I want off.'"

This is a much harder decision to make if the person is unconscious or victim of a stroke, especially if this is someone who has been treated at the hospital for ten or fifteen years. "They're almost like family," Rutsky says. "We feel a strong commitment to these people. But what do you do?"

Rutsky admits there are times when he is led by his emotions. "God, he's too nice a guy," Rutsky says. "I'm going to give him a chance even though his odds are very poor, and even though all logical facts point to a very poor outcome. You say to yourself, 'There's a ten or twenty percent chance he'll do all right. That's better than no chance.' So, you go ahead and put him on dialysis. It turns out you were dead right. He does terribly. He's miserable. What do you do with them? I find it very hard to continue to provide care to these people when it's hopeless. When it's clear that there's no hope. I try very hard to help them make a decision to stop if it's clear they're going nowhere. The majority of these peo-ple cannot make that decision."

There are times though when Rutsky gets what he calls an intuitive sense about a patient, and the results are quite different. He can look at a patient, telling the family there's less than a 20 percent chance of recovery, but then say that providing no further catastrophes arise, he can see no reason why the patient couldn't get better.

"We just discharged a man," Rutsky says. "He was admitted six months ago. He tried to burn some fire ants with gasoline and lit himself on fire instead. He had third-degree burns over more than fifty percent of his body. He developed acute renal failure and was on a ventilator for a long time. We managed him, dia-lyzed him daily, and four months later he recovered kidney func-tion. He'll walk out of here alive. When that guy first came here, I just felt he was going to survive. He hadn't recovered his renal functions yet. He still had burns that needed grafting. He had to be fed by intravenous line requiring huge amounts of protein and calories. He had the opportunity of dying from infection daily," Rutsky recalls. But in spite of his severe health problems, "I just knew he was going to make it."

Outside of making diagnoses, Rutsky feels the real art of medicine, the intuitive judgment element, "is learning when to do the right thing, or when not to do the right thing. So much of medicine is knowing when to withhold therapy. Doctors feel uncomfortable doing nothing, but there are many illnesses that get better with a minimum of therapy. Part of my judgment as a good physician is knowing when to let well enough alone. Let the body heal itself. It does a far better job than most doctors can."

An age-old axiom of business is that decisions should be made only when they have to be. Management expert Peter Drucker likens decision making to surgery. "It is an intervention into a sys-tem and therefore carries with it the risk of shock. One does not make unnecessary decisions any more than a good surgeon does unnecessary surgery."

Heisenberg's uncertainty principle takes that idea a step further. The mere observation of subatomic particles affects their behavior. In other words, in the makeup of universal matter, there is no passive observation, only active participation. This is a profound metaphor for all decision makers. A doctor's intrusion into a patient, running tests, poking into areas that don't need poking, can turn up irrelevant facts and lead a doctor away from his original diagnosis toward another direction that could very well cause the death of the patient.

"Doctors indeed make mistakes that end up in the death of patients," Rutsky says. "I know I have. But those mistakes are sometimes not out of malpractice, not out of negligence, but out of a pursuit of information that seems relevant to the patient's care and survival. It's like bad intelligence at war time. You act on it if you've gone ahead and gotten it. But sometimes you ignore it, though you may be ignoring it at the patient's peril. We're not talking about decisions to put fertilizer on your garden. Who gives a damn if the garden doesn't grow in the end? We're talking about is the patient going to die or not because of what you've done?"

These are patients, Rutsky points out, who can die at any time. "They're beyond their appointed time, and their bodies are not like normal people's. That's the pressure I'm under as a nephrologist. It gets to me more than anything else."

Very few patients have textbook symptom complexes. Rutsky believes that "The truly exceptional physician is able to synthesize and integrate the facts, his knowledge base, and experience, and from that be able to come up with a diagnosis that is in part logical deduction and in part intuitive. It is truly the great physician who can make the jump, who goes beyond the algorithms to the correct choice."

Lewis Goldfrank stands tall in that group. He is a man who puts his innate synthesizing abilities on the line day in and day out. Rarely do people in business have to deal with the level of calamitous decision making encountered by Goldfrank and Rutsky. How do they cope with the constant flow of catastrophe that they must confront on a daily basis?

"There has to be a balance," Goldfrank says, "and how people achieve that balance is critical." Goldfrank would never make it if he felt that he had to save every alcoholic or substance abuser he saw. But it is the occasional save that keeps him at it. He points up to a bottle of Night Train Express wine on his book-cluttered shelf. "I had a guy give me that bottle of Night Train. He brought it to me because he was an alcoholic that we convinced to get off alcohol and [who] actually quit. He's a marker. Maybe one out of twenty people we see who have terrible problems are going to succeed. But that might be very substantial. If five percent of the alcoholics we see get into a program, we stop them from drinking, then they no longer abuse their spouse, they don't drive a car and create another catastrophe, then I've made some progress. If we allow that one kid to get through school, or one other pregnancy survives without fetal alcohol syndrome, that gives me a measure of success. You have to believe that you can accomplish things other people doubt. You have to believe in the unbelievable. That's the way to keep a steady keel in the midst of what seems to be chaos. It's nothing new. Lewis Carroll had the Queen say to Alice, 'You've got to think one unbelievable thing before breakfast every day.' I've got to believe that I can solve problems that others have said are insolvable."

13

ACTIVATING WHAT YOU KNOW

In an uncertain world there are no neat formulas of programmed sequence of steps that guarantees successful outcomes.

R. PIKE

JIM BRAGINGTON BUILDS telescopes. He calls these large mirrored
amateur telescopes "Odysseys." They are built in a simple fashion
based on the designs of Frank Dobson using materials like sinotubes for the telescope's tube assembly. Sinotubes are large, tough
cardboard tubes normally used as molds for concrete pillars. Coul-
ter's telescopes are made for one thing: viewing the heavens up
close with human eyes. By most modern telescope standards these
telescopes are crude. They lack an equatorial mount, which means
they cannot be aligned with the movement of the earth to track a
deep sky object like a distant galaxy—a necessity for astrophotog-
raphy. These telescopes are also unable to be automatically set to
ascension and declension coordinates, which points telescopes in
the exact direction of these distant deep sky objects, such as star
clusters or wispy nebulae.

The only way to locate these celestial beauties with one of Bragington's Odysseys is to know in which constellation and direction they lie. The telescope is then nudged around to that distant area until the object is found.

One of the most stunning of these deep sky objects is called the Ring Nebula. It is known as a planetary nebula. This is a misnomer because the gas cloud (nebula) it describes has nothing to do with planets. The Ring Nebula is actually the gaseous remnants of a star that exploded, leaving a relatively small smoke ring about fifteen hundred light years away. It is invisible to the naked eye or a pair of binoculars. But Bragington can look up in the sky and point to the constellation Lyra, direct a viewer to a pair of stars, one on top of the other, and say with certainty, "even though you can't see it, it's there."

Then guiding his large telescope with its thirteen-inch mirror, referred to as a light bucket by amateur astronomers, Bragington points the telescope skyward. There are no guide marks other than Bragington's knowledge, experience, and inner vision that says there is something where nothing can be seen. He steps away from the eyepiece, and another viewer steps forward. There in the center of this mirrored image is the tiny smoke ring hovering in the vastness of our galaxy, suspended against a backdrop of heavenly glitter. This shining ring, lit by the stars behind it, is all that is left of a star destroyed ages ago.

Stepping back from the eyepiece, the viewer looks to the sky. All he can see are the crowded glimmers of distant stars. There is no clue as to either the location or existence of this astronomical body. But Bragington has been there before; he's found this nebula hundreds of times. He knows that when he points his scope between those two stars in Lyra, he will find this hidden night sky jewel.

Discovering the inner intuitive source is much like Bragington's probing of the heavens. Because if you have been there before, directed by another person or having found it by yourself, you can return to it again and again. Since it is invisible to the naked eye, you have to know where to look before you can start finding it at will.

The ancients thought the heavens were filled with magic. Comets were harbingers of doom. Like these primitive impressions, intuition also seemed magical because of its special qualities. Now we know differently. Comets are met with excitement and anticipation. The same is happening to our relationship to the inner thought processes that once seemed so mysterious and distant.

There have always been those who have had a sense of the universe and have sought to dispel the mystery. So too with intuition: We have always had those people who trust this source. For a time, they may have done so silently. Like Copernicus, who feared that his revelations of the nature of our solar system would ostracize him, decision makers who have trusted their intuition have kept quiet out of fear of disapproval by society. In many cases, however, the courage to continue trusting that source has lifted these people beyond the mass of mystic mockers and conventional wisdom purveyors into the role of successful leaders.

Taking the intuitive leap is often a courageous step. During the reign of the Roman Emperor Caligula, the personal slave of a noble Roman countryman escaped into the countryside. His name was Androcles. Bolting from his master was a rather bold decision. He knew he'd be hunted down. His only hope was to hide out for a while and hope that things would eventually quiet down.

Androcles thought his dream had been answered when he stumbled on a cave in search of berries. It was a perfect hideout. The mouth of the cave was well shielded from the path. Within yards grew a rambling berry bush on the banks of a stream. Androcles marched into the cave without a care only to be met by the roar of a ferocious lion. "Great," Androcles thought, "I'm finally free and now I'm lunch." Meeting this lion was not part of his original plan. But then, as mentioned earlier, planning is everything, plans are nothing.

The lion roared wildly. Androcles suddenly had an image that something else was going on here. He heard something that made him think, "The beast doth protest too much." Androcles was right. When the lion raised its paw, Androcles saw what was the real problem. Sticking out of the lion's clawed paw was a thorn that had driven its way into the tender flesh.

Androcles's fear lowered and he spoke to the lion soothingly, assuring the beast that he knew the thorn was really why he was so angry. Androcles proposed a deal. "I'll remove the thorn, but if I do, you'll let me go." The lion agreed to the terms.

Having no desire to be caught unaware—experience had taught him lions weren't always up to their word—Androcles moved cautiously toward the lion's inflamed paw. Gently, he took hold of it and plucked out the offending sticker. The lion roared.

As the lion approached, Androcles retreated into the cave. A curious thing happened. The lion, rather than devouring Androcles, started rubbing up against him like a big kitten.

With a sigh of relief, Androcles made his farewells and took off for safer ground. Unfortunately, he escaped right back into the grasp of his master's henchmen. His fate and punishment: to be thrown to the lions at the upcoming games.

According to Roman historian Aulus Gullius, when the day of the games arrived, Androcles was placed in the center of the coliseum, the door swung open, and out charged the lion. Androcles could not believe what he saw. The lion he now stood face to face with was none other than his patient in the cave. Androcles, to the roar of the crowd, strode confidently up to the lion and began to pet him. The audience was so overwhelmed by Androcles's courage and ability that he and the lion were freed from their bonds.

Often the images that prevail in business are those of the warrior: the hero, who by sheer might has conquered the enemy. St. George, who has slain the dragon. In many ways the stories of Androcles and St. George are two sides of a decision maker. One side sees the beast as an object to be destroyed. The other side knows that the only way to survive rests in the decision maker's ability to relate to the beast. It's the reconciliation of these two sides, without ignoring either aspect, that leads to successful decisions. R. E. McMaster spoke about this same idea he called "truth in tension." A decision maker will be successful over the long run only when these two distinct halves can be held in mutually constructive action. This is the composite picture, open to all options, assessments, directions, and values.

In his study of senior managers for the *Harvard Business Review*, Daniel Isenberg suggested that one way a decision maker can bring this total picture into focus is to stress the importance of values, preferences, and the use of imagination.

The connection between intuition, imagination, and creativity has always been strong. Creativity often marks the difference between those who lead the way and those who only manage. This means that those managers who wish to rise within the organizational structure need to develop leadership qualities above and beyond their managerial abilities. They need to be willing to open themselves to more creative approaches, which requires intuition. Unlocking the door to the intuitive opens the manager to the realm of possibilities, the birthplace of creativity.

This need is especially true for lower and middle management. Studies by Isenberg and Weston Agor have shown that upper management demonstrates a greater and more successful use of intuition than their associates. If leaders are interested in raising the level of decision making with their organizations, it is up to them to foster creative behavior in those who work for them. As mentioned earlier, creativity and intelligence are equally distributed throughout an organization. When the whole organization is thinking creatively, not just the leader, innovation takes off and profits rise.

Practice is the key. Practice increases fluency, and fluency leads to more willing flexibility. Isenberg recommends that managers improve their intuitive fluency by developing skills at mapping unfamiliar areas by generalizing facts and then testing the generalizations against more facts.

Visualizing and building scenarios is an excellent approach. This step-by-step outline is an imaginary scripting of a decision. The decision maker plots out what will happen from the moment the decision is made to a point in the future. Every roadblock, problem, and potential reaction is visualized and recorded. The more detail applied to this step-by-step outline, the better the decision that will follow it.

A corporate culture that encourages and demands this kind of creative thinking builds decisions in which the options are illuminated and then given life. This breeds confidence in decision makers at every level in an organization. They feel that their ventures into their inner thought processes are a valued and meaningful aspect of an organization's success. This kind of recognition also helps to bond the lower-level decision makers with the organization. It makes them feel like a vital part of the process in a fashion that the purely analytical decision could never hope to accomplish.

As with learning any new approach, the first steps taken are to make the process conscious. Improving intuition requires that the steps be made visible. As decision makers' intuitive comfort level rises and they become more competent with the process of trusting what they know, they will be able to bypass many levels of painstaking analysis.

Trusting what makes you feel comfortable may seem like an irrational, unscientific approach to decision making, but scientists and social scientists are reassessing their theories on how people know. What they have found is that people learn best along the lines of what has always felt most natural for both the teacher and the learner. In other words, the rational approach to making decisions is to be comfortable and find your comfort level.

Getting comfortable in a highly competitive, highly pressured global marketplace doesn't require complete relaxation. Some decision makers thrive on the hurried and hectic daily pace. It's at those times when they're so busy that they can't possibly sit down and analyze a situation that they come up with their best decisions. But Ira Glasser's warning should be repeated. If you aren't loaded with the right information, your inner processor is capable of throwing out bad choices. Intuition is only as good as the knowledge and experience that feeds it.

Joseph Chilton Pearce said, "We act our way into believing and we believe our way into acting." If Pearce's viewpoint is correct, then trusting and valuing the intuitive sense becomes an act that is not only the guiding force of decision makers but also the glue that holds the process together.

Actively implementing intuition allows a decision maker to focus on the long-term, away from the quarterly report mentality. The pressure of the short-term keeps a decision maker from the vision necessary to lead an organization forward. Where would Apple be if John Sculley didn't have a future vision of the possibilities available to his company? It probably would never have grown beyond the chaos left behind by its brilliant but relatively inexperienced founders. Would we be confronting a different Soviet threat if Pete Dailey hadn't seen how to communicate the big picture to the leaders and people of Europe? By including and valuing the intuitive, decision makers move toward a complete system, preparing them for the rapid changes to come.

Singularly, one of the most transforming big pictures the world has ever seen was a shot provided by the ill-fated *Apollo 13* astronauts on their way home from the moon. It was a picture of the earth as a full globe. In one illuminating flash, people saw the reality and power of the whole picture.

The image of that picture cannot be destroyed. It has entered the culture. It has been imprinted onto the modern worldview. The human race saw itself from a perspective that no other generation had ever seen before.

Acting on that big picture image of the global system means actively and consciously incorporating the intuitive process into the system. By doing this, it opens up a whole new door of options for action. The world becomes the playing stage, and the decisions reflect that perspective. It means we must become more responsible in addressing major, long-range decisions.

If success is the quest, a complete picture is needed. One example of real success comes from former Washington Redskins football coach Joe Gibbs. In Super Bowl XVII, Washington is seconds from victory, and Gibbs has moved down the row of players about to charge onto the field to celebrate their super achievement. He is looking for his son among the throng of revelers. He finds him in the melee, and places his arm around his boy. They share the moment of the final ticks of the clock together. It was a rare and special moment for Gibbs, where he felt his real success was as much the moment of victory as the sharing.

This is a picture of a decision maker becoming a whole person, functioning on all levels of awareness, and not missing what is truly important for a quick and only partial success.

Using the whole brain, the whole body, and relating it to the whole world perspective places a decision maker in a role filled with options—for success and for failure. Without the options there can be no possibility for growth and development, which is the long-range goal of the species. Being alert to the intonations of the intuitive process is a matter of listening. It is relating to the beast, as Androcles did, rather than trying to slay it. Sometimes there is no other choice but to use the sword. Knowing when not to use it, however, is the mark of understanding and even greater success. When that choice is made successfully, even the beast profits.

Intuition is options, not answers. Once the possibilities are clear, as the decision makers interviewed in this book have shown, the answers come. It may take a trusting leap, or it may take only a receptive ear. Whatever it takes, those who listen to their intuition are changing the world.

14

EXERCISING THE INTUITIVE MIND

"Excuse me sir, can you tell me how to get to Carnegie Hall?"

"Practice, kid. Practice."

FLUENCY IN ANY undertaking requires practice. This is true whether we're learning a new language, a child is learning to walk, or a student is learning multiplication tables. We improve by repeating the process over and over.

The exercises that follow have been designed and tested to allow decision makers to prime and practice their intuition. If your intuition is already strong, you can use these exercises to deepen your abilities.

Following the exercises, in the Appendix is a copy of the Gray-Wheelwright Jungian Type Survey (personality test). This is a generalized measurement of certain psychological factors that point the way to a person's perceived way of processing information. It is not exact and should be taken only as a road map, but it is a guide to understanding a portion of a person's personality.

183

INTUITIVE EXERCISE 1

One fairly easy technique for unlocking intuition is relaxation—learning to sit quietly and let go of a pressing issue. This period can be as short as five minutes and can take place while seated in a chair or even under the spray of a showerhead. It can also be a formalized process such as taking twenty minutes a day to meditate.

Relaxation is the release mode, which is needed to free the mind from the conscious overlays of thought and analysis. This process of letting go quiets the conscious activity, allowing the decision maker to listen to the voices of the inner process. As Frances Vaughan explains in her book, *Awakening Intuition*, "You are learning to listen to what you already know, but in order to hear, your mind must be quiet rather than full of the things you think you need to learn."

At first, this exercise may seem like a waste of valuable time, a great indulgence, especially when facing urgent matters. But by allowing yourself even a short amount of time to quietly strip off the superficial conscious layers that tend to block access to your inner processor, you provide yourself the opportunity for true reflection.

One of the easiest methods of relaxation is breath awareness. Simply listen to the pattern of your breathing. If you find yourself drifting away from concentrating on your breathing patterns into other concerns, bring yourself back to the breathing.

To some, there may be great resistance to trying even the most basic of these exercises. The thought might be, "My God, what would happen if somebody walked in and saw me like this? They'd think I was some kind of mystic kook." If these are legitimate concerns, start behind closed doors. The real trick to unlocking intuition is to start. Once the initial resistance has been hurdled, the process becomes easier.

Relaxing the body and listening to the intuitive voices also means listening to the rhythms and cues the body gives you. For some, this is a rich time when they can realize body reactions in ways they might never have experienced them before.

Once the mind has been able to relax for even the shortest of times, the material locked inside is freed. Remember, intuition is a quiet voice often overpowered by more "rational" voices. But if you don't take the time to listen, how can you ever expect to hear?

INTUITIVE EXERCISE 2

Listening to the intuitive voice is often a process of not censoring the information being brought to consciousness. This exercise relies on your ability to not censor yourself. Using either a pad of paper or a computer, quiet yourself and get a picture in your mind of a person who has had a profound, positive effect on your life: a teacher, a mentor, or perhaps a counselor. To yourself, ask this person, "What is it about me that you like?" Then write down, without censoring, exactly what you hear. This is a process of letting go of your conscious controls. You remain in charge of the process, but are not to control the information you receive. When the voice has completed its thoughts, ask, "What do I still need to learn from you?" Again, write down exactly what you hear. This process of active imagination is a very powerful tool for unlocking intuition. It is not a game, and it is important to remember that even though you are letting go of the control, you are still in charge of yourself. (Being in charge and not in control is often the difference between a leader and a boss.) The more you use and practice these techniques, the easier it will be to hear, recognize, and not censor the quiet voice of intuition.

INTUITIVE EXERCISE 3

Brainstorming is an excellent group intuitive building exercise for people with a common goal. Brainstorming requires nothing more than a flip chart and a marker. Its purpose is to help a group of people come up with as many ideas as possible in a short period of time. The procedures are simple. Once a problem or scenario is before the group, it should be written down at the top of a flip chart. Then participants contribute ideas for solving the problem.

It is imperative that the person writing down the ideas write down every idea that is spoken. No idea is left off the initial brainstorm, nor is any idea judged or criticized. The group is encouraged to speak as the ideas occur, without waiting to be called upon. Brainstorming sessions are kept short, around five to ten minutes in length. Once all the ideas are on the flip chart sheets, the group then prioritizes the entries. The first prioritization is made with "ones" and "twos." A one is a higher priority item. A two is not as high. If all the items on the list are ones, simply move on to the next step in the process, which is to prioritize the entries listed as one more critically, but without passing any personally critical judgment on the ideas.

Brainstorming needs to be in an environment where people feel safe to speak up, encouraging them to listen to their intuitive impulses and make them known. Then, by writing every idea spoken on the chart, every idea is honored. People feel successful, valued, and even willing to see their ideas receive a lower priority rather than simply being rejected out of hand. This process stimulates more intuitive ideas.

INTUITIVE EXERCISE 4

You might think that letting go to a decision and allowing it to resolve itself is a luxury when a decision needs to be made immediately—but forcing a decision might also prove costly. One approach is to focus on a decision prior to going to sleep, letting go of it, and waking up to an answer.

Before retiring for the night, sit in a quiet place and take a few deep breaths. Then allow yourself to focus or visualize the decision you need to make. Don't try to resolve any conflicts, just let yourself think about the decision. Then say to yourself, "I would like an answer to this decision when I awake." Take a few more deep breaths and release the image. If you are having trouble letting go of the decision, visualize a favorite vacation spot and take yourself there. This exercise requires that you have confidence in your abilities and trust that you know what you know. Upon rising in the morning, ask yourself "What decision should I make?" Listen carefully to the response you hear within yourself and write it down.

INTUITIVE EXERCISE 5

Cray Research's John Rollwagen suggested two exercises in chapter 3 that bear repeating. First was his visualization exercise, in which you find a quiet space, visualize the past year and what has taken place throughout the year to bring you where you are today. Now, visualize where you want to be at the end of the next year, and carefully visualize a pathway back to where you are today. As Rollwagen explained, this exercise should not be followed step-by-step but as an indication of possible routes forward.

His second exercise suggestion is to use a coin toss to make a decision. The point here is not necessarily to use the actual outcome but to carefully observe the reaction you have toward the results. The reaction will tell you what you're really thinking.

INTUITIVE EXERCISE 6

This day-long exercise is designed to help you recognize and capture your intuitive impulses. Using a small pocket notebook, simply write down every intuitive flash (or what you perceive as an intuitive flash) that arises during a given day. Do not censor any of these ideas; just record them. These may include: standing in one line versus another at the market; switching lanes while driving (don't write this one down until you get off the road); a sudden urge to bring flowers to the person you love; a sudden urge to pick up a magazine you don't normally buy; or the name of a person you hadn't thought of in a while. The exercise here is only to note the impulse. Following through on any of them is up to you. If you do follow one, make sure to write down the outcome.

At the end of the day, go back through the notebook and count how many times you consciously had an intuitive impulse. The rest of the week try and be aware of your intuitive voice. A week or so later, try the exercise again. Check against the last list. Chances are you'll notice an increase in the sheer number of intuitive impulses, and you'll probably also find that the impulses are more accurately in tune with your needs.

INTUITIVE EXERCISE 7

The card game Concentration is an excellent intuition builder. If you have children, it is also a way to discern their intuitive capabilities as well as have some fun. Using a deck of cards, spread the cards face up in four rows of 13. Immediately, go back and turn the cards over. Now, trusting what you know, play the game. Once you've flipped over all the matches you remember, begin to allow yourself the opportunity to let go to a card's position. If you're playing with children, watch how they let go and make some amazing connections. This is not a test of ESP, but rather an exercise that encourages you to stretch the limits of what you know.

INTUITIVE EXERCISE 8

Sit in a quiet place. Close your eyes and breathe normally. Visualize the smallest particle you can imagine. Then visualize the particle increasing in size to the size of a pea, then to the size of a baseball, a basketball, a giant snowball, a massive boulder, an entire city, the planet earth, the solar system, the entire galaxy, and then a group of galaxies. Move beyond that into complete darkness. When you are within the darkness, ask yourself, "What big picture do I need to see?" Make sure you record the first image that comes to you even if it makes no sense to you at the time. It probably will in the near future.

INTUITIVE EXERCISE 9

Sit in a quiet place. Close your eyes and breathe normally. Visualize the entrance to a cave. Walk into the cave. On the left is a doorway. Walk through the door. On the other side you will see a landscape. Slowly look over the landscape and you will see an animal. Go to the animal and ask it to take you to your guide. When the animal has taken you to your guide, ask the guide if he or she is truly your guide. If the person says no, ask the animal to take you to your guide again. When the guide answers yes to your question, step back and take a good look at your guide, noting clothing and facial features. Ask the guide's name, then ask the guide to tell you what he or she needs to tell you. Ask the guide to give you a symbol that you can take back with you. If you don't understand the significance of the symbol, ask your guide to explain it. Thank your guide for the symbol and ask what you need to do for him or her. When you have received this information, ask where you can meet your guide again. Then return through the door in the cave. Open your eyes. You can return to this place any time you wish, and your guide will answer any questions you may have. If your guide is unable to answer your question, he or she can take you to someone who can.

By practicing these exercises, we begin the listening process. As has been said throughout this book, leadership is a matter of listening. It is actively listening to oneself, to those working for the leader, and to the world at large. Intuitive leadership arises when the leader is capable of creating a culture that nurtures and encourages creative and innovative ideas throughout an organization.

How does a leader create a culture open to creativity, innovation, and the intuitive? By recognizing that people are capable of creative and innovative solutions to problems, if given the opportunity to solve them. Everyone in an organization has a head, a mouth, and a heart.

The vast majority of people that come to work do so because they want to do a good job. Providing them with an environment that fosters their participation, having weekly brainstorming meetings that allow them to solve problems at their root cause, and then quickly implementing their ideas, works wonders. Empowerment to solve problems at the source means a leader has to let go of some control, facilitating solutions, not imposing them.

Intuitive leadership is not making every decision or solving every problem that arises within an organization. It is up to the leader to develop and champion the company vision, making sure that everyone within the organization shares that vision. It is out of this big picture that an organization produces a context for its decisions.

Intuitive leadership also requires a willingness to make, admit, and accept mistakes. It's important to mention, however, that a leader is not expected to excuse mistakes caused by slovenly work habits or poor practices. It's the mistake generated by aspiration that should be forgiven and acknowledged. When people within an organization believe they can be innovative and possibly fail without suffering any recriminations, then creativity and intuition begin to flourish.

The ability to hear the intuitive voice when it arises is purely one of exercise, preparation, and practice. The ability to trust it only comes by acting on it. As long as we are tied to the conventional wisdom that counsels safety over risk, we will never be able to step outside and reach the stars. The intuitive leader knows that in a competitive world the status quo inspires few and creates less. It is only by stretching beyond what can be seen, and listening to the quiet voice, that real innovation and growth is possible. That is the realm of the intuitive.

JUNGIAN TYPE SURVEY

HORACE GRAY, M.D.

JANE H. WHEELWRIGHT

JOSEPH B. WHEELWRIGHT, M.D.

DIRECTIONS

This is a study of *psychological types*, not of intelligence or emotion. There are no right or wrong answers. Everybody has each tendency at times. Which do you use most readily; i. e., which best describes your natural, spontaneous, or typical tendency, as distinguished from how you may wish to be and from what you have made of yourself?

Please mark your answers on the separate answer sheet. Answers are both easier and more satisfactory if run off in twenty minutes, skipping any you don't like; then if you care to reread and change any, do so.

1. In general company do you like to
   a. Listen
   b. Talk

2. In viewing a problem, do you
   a. First seek a background of experience
   b. First appraise the particular time-place-person

3. Is your nature more to
   a. Think and feel about life
   b. Throw yourself into active experience

4. Are you more interested in
   a. Why a person is the way he is
   b. Why he does something

5. Assuming your living were assured, would you follow a vocation
   a. On the imaginative side
   b. On the useful side

6. Do you like pictures with a sense of
   a. Soaring upward
   b. Closeness to earth

7. In practice, are you
   a. Casual
   b. Punctual

8. Granting that you are tactful in practice, what is your real impulse
   a. Speak out
   b. Noncommittal

9. In forming judgments, is your mental process mainly
   a. To look for a guiding principle
   b. To declare your personal valuation

10. In study of mankind, do you prefer
    a. Principles and laws
    b. Manners and valuations

11. Do you express yourself more easily in
    a. Writing
    b. Conversation

12. Do you wonder what is behind people's remarks
    a. Often
    b. Not much

13. Eager to join in others' plans
    a. Seldom
    b. Usually

14. Do you prefer to
    a. Read about a thing
    b. Hear about a thing

15. Is your impulse to be
    a. Leisurely
    b. Punctual

16. When a book is disappointing do you
    a. Try a new one
    b. Finish it anyway

17. When about to travel, do you pack up
    a. At the last moment
    b. At leisure

18. Mostly, do you prefer people with
    a. Good thinking
    b. Good feeling

19. Is it easier to devote yourself to
    a. Social problems
    b. Friends' problems

20. Is tact to you a matter of
    a. Respecting independent views
    b. Warm sympathy

21. In giving praise are you
    a. Reserved
    b. Outspoken

22. Is your attitude becoming
    a. More general
    b. More specific

23. Do you like to chat with clerks, hairdressers, porters, etc.
    a. No
    b. Yes

24. Is the telephone bell a pleasure
    a. No
    b. Yes

25. Do you overlook details because of immediate interests
    a. Rather often
    b. Seldom

26. In reading, do you prefer
    a. Poetry and fantasy
    b. Current events

27. In perceiving things, is your first approach
    a. General effect
    b. Important details

28. In reasoning, do you proceed from
    a. General rule to particular case
    b. Particular case to general rule

29. Confronted with misfortunes in others is your impulse to
    a. Search for the cause
    b. Console

30. When you overhear 2 persons in a difference of opinion do you hope
    a. Something good comes out of this
    b. They will stop it

31. How many friends do you have
    a. Few
    b. Many

32. Regarding human reactions, are you interested more in
    a. General psychic laws
    b. Individual peculiarities

33. In reading do you prefer
    a. Character study
    b. Action

34. In color designs do you prefer
    a. Muted effects
    b. Gay effects

35. Do you spend or save
    a. Spend
    b. Save

36. Is orderliness
    a. A bother
    b. A cinch

37. Do you size up a person on basis of a very short interview
    a. Yes
    b. No

38. When your opinions vary from those of your circle are you
    a. Intrigued
    b. Uncomfortable

39. Are you more interested in people's
    a. Beliefs
    b. Behavior

40. Do you take observations as facts
    a. To be studied
    b. To be valued for use

41. On which side is your temperament
    a. Deliberate
    b. Spontaneous

42. In personal letters do you tend to
    a. Alter words here and there
    b. Let it go as first written

43. Do you enjoy meeting strange people
    a. No
    b. Yes

44. At home are you conversational
    a. Not very
    b. Rather

45. On vacation do you act mostly on
    a. Spur of the moment
    b. According to plan

46. Do conclusions come to you by
    a. Immediate inspiration
    b. Deliberate reasoning

47. If living alone would you
    a. Not bother much with details
    b. Keep things in precise order

48. When you meet people, do you prefer to discuss their
    a. Profession
    b. Personal tastes

49. In reading do you prefer
    a. Biography
    b. Novels

50. Do you prefer the entrance to a building
    a. Small
    b. Large

51. At a party are you happier with
    a. Six
    b. Dozen

52. When abed for a week or more, provided household and business are well taken care of, are you restless
    a. No
    b. Yes

53. Would you rather have friends around
    a. 1 night, alone 6
    b. 3 nights, alone 4

54. When a person has a wrong idea, do you
    a. Change the subject
    b. Try to convert him

55. Does a problem seem like a closed room which intuition has to open
    a. Quite frequently
    b. Not much

56. In works of art, do you prefer mainly

a. Generalized
b. Photographic

57. Is neatness in you
    a. An achievement
    b. Inborn

58. Suppose you were waiting in a hotel with two lobbies, each in good taste in different colors, which would you choose to wait in
    a. Blues
    b. Reds

59. Toward goals once chosen, are you
    a. Tenacious
    b. Readily reoriented

60. Do you like making collections
    a. Yes
    b. No

61. Granting you like both, which do you prefer most of the time
    a. Reflective people
    b. Lively people

62. In pictures, which attracts you more
    a. Form
    b. Color

63. Do you prefer to make decisions
    a. At leisure
    b. Immediately

64. Assuming equal familiarity, would you prefer to go to the theater to see

a. Hamlet
b. Romeo and Juliet

65. Are you unaccountably restless
    a. From time to time
    b. Rarely

66. When sleepless, do you take a pill
    a. Off and on
    b. Rarely

67. Before a spring landscape, are you more aware of
    a. General lines and coloring
    b. Details of sky, trees, flowers

68. Do you draw out people on
    a. Their special interests
    b. Miscellaneous things

69. In reading for information, do you prefer the presentation
    a. Sustained and thorough
    b. Many-sided and mobile

70. Do you tend to develop
    a. Inner life
    b. Outer life

71. Do you like to be occupied with
    a. One thing at a time
    b. A variety of things

72. Eager that others join your plans
    a. Sometimes
    b. Usually

73. In room decoration, do you prefer
    a. Earthy tones
    b. Primary colors

74. Are you tempted to new pursuits
    a. Quite a bit
    b. Not much

75. When picking a present for somebody, do you seek something
    a. You think will be a pleasant surprise
    b. You think he wants

76. Were you born with a time clock in your mind
    a. No
    b. Yes

77. What style of art do you prefer
    a. Traditional
    b. Modernist

78. Is your temperament
    a. Serious
    b. Cheerful

79. Do you
    a. Restrict your friends to a few with whom you are then relatively confidential
    b. Have many amicable relationships

80. Having formed an opinion, do you
    a. Alter it willingly
    b. Tend to stick

81. With regard to future possibilities do you
    a. Cross bridges as they come
    b. Plan for various contingencies

THE SURVEY

The Jungian Type Survey is a psychological survey that is designed to delineate types of personality structure. In his book, *Psychological Types*, published in 1921, Dr. Jung defined and described the attitudes and functions that form specific personality types.

First is the general attitude of the individual; Introversion versus Extraversion. According as psychic energy is habitually directed inward or outward. Next may be taken the paired functions of perception: sensation versus intuition. Then come the two functions of judgment: thinking versus feeling.

The purpose of the survey is to provide a psychological-type description of the person who fills out the questionnaire.

ADMINISTRATION

The administration of the test is simple. The examinee is given the booklet and an answer sheet, with instructions to read each question and record his answer in the appropriate place on the answer sheet. The suggested time is twenty minutes and the emphasis is on first reaction to the question rather than prolonged consideration of it. The items on the answer sheet are numbered vertically rather than horizontally, and it is perhaps well to ascertain that the examinee is aware of this before he starts marking his answers.

SCORING

The scoring is done on six scales. These are:

I. Introversion
E. Extraversion
U. Intuition
S. Sensation
T. Thinking
F. Feeling

In the scoring process, the answer sheet is viewed as being constructed in a horizontal pattern. The numbers of the first ten questions now also designate the ten lines into which the answer sheet is divided. Lines 1 through 4 are the Introversion-Extraversion Scale, while lines 5 through 7 represent the Intuition-Sensation Scale, and lines 8 through 10 record the Thinking-Feeling Scale.

The number of (a) answers in lines 1 through 4 are counted and recorded under I (Introversion); the number of (b) answers in the same lines are recorded under E (Extraversion). In lines 5 through 7 the (a) answers are recorded under U (Intuition), while the (b) answers are under S (Sensation). In lines 8 through 10 the (a) answers are listed under T (Thinking), while the (b) answers are listed under F (Feeling). There are thirty-four questions on the

I–E Scale, twenty-six questions on the U–S Scale, and twenty-one questions on the T–F Scale.

After recording the scores in the spaces provided at the lower right of the scoring sheet, a pictorial representation may be made by plotting them on the graphs following the scoring page. This is done by placing the numerical scores at the appropriate places on the gradated lines that indicate the area tested. This profile not only gives an immediate representation of the psychological type, but also shows which of the four functions in the Extraverted or Introverted personality is the primary function, and what places are assigned to the other three functions in the personality.

VALIDITY AND RELIABILITY

The validity of the test is at best difficult to verify. There is no pre- and postcondition, nor progress in treatment, nor firm conviction against which to evaluate test results.

Perhaps the best indication of validity is the concept of face validity; namely it is valid insofar as it appears to be valid. The original questions of the survey were conceived by a student of Jung, Dr. Joseph B. Wheelwright; Jane H. Wheelwright, also a student of Jung; and Dr. Horace Gray. Help and criticism were given by Dr. Joseph Henderson. All of the authors are Jungian analysts.

Differing ways in which people of the various psychological types responded to others and the world around them were incorporated into questions. Some of these blatantly pull for one type of reaction rather than another (i.e., do you enjoy meeting strange people?) and some are more subtle (i.e., do you prefer good yellows or good greens?) These questions were then posed to people who had been previously clinically typed by the authors of the test. When it was found that the answers agreed with the clinical impression, they were retained in the battery. When they disagreed, they were eliminated. In this way, eighty-one items have been retained in the present revision (number 15), all of which are in agreement with the original clinical impression of type. Each item to be included in the battery met the criterion of being associated with a clinical impression of Introversion-Extraversion, sensa-tion-intuition, thinking-feeling to the extent of P 05 or less, when computed by one degree of freedom chi square.

The reliability of the test has not been established by split-half or by test-retest methods. Such work is currently being undertaken.

In any event it is to be noted that the authors are not of the belief that the test has been adequately standardized and would say that such statistical standardization is not possible until the validation criteria are more fully established.

THE PROFILE

There are three bipolar scales that are measured; the Introver-sion-Extraversion, the Intuition-Sensation, and the Thinking-Feeling scales. The basic scale is the Introversion-Extraversion that shows the general attitude or direction of mental energy. Then there is the function by which the person perceives the world about him, the Intuition-Sensation scale. Finally, there is the judging function, Thinking-Feeling, by which the person sizes up his perceptions.

The first scale, then, shows whether the subject is introverted or extraverted, and the following two scales show which of the two functions he most frequently uses. This gives us eight possible variables.

Introvert, with Intuition and Feeling
Introvert, with Intuition and Thinking
Introvert, with Sensation and Feeling
Introvert, with Sensation and Thinking
Extravert, with Intuition and Feeling
Extravert, with Intuition and Thinking
Extravert, with Sensation and Feeling
Extravert, with Sensation and Thinking

The survey has a further refinement in that it measures the pri-macy of the perception or judging function. Granted that a person has been shown to be (for example) an Extraverted-Intuitive-Feeling type, it then remains to determine whether he exercises the function in that order, or whether the order should be reversed and the feeling function take primacy.

This gives a division of types into sixteen permutations and provides a category of basic personality types into which everyone falls.

For ease of reference, the sixteen variables are listed here, divided under the general attitude heading of Introversion and Extraversion.

Introversion	Extraversion
Intuitive-Feeling	Intuitive-Feeling
Feeling-Intuitive	Feeling-Intuitive
Intuitive-Thinking	Intuitive-Thinking
Thinking-Intuitive	Thinking-Intuitive
Sensation-Feeling	Sensation-Feeling
Feeling-Sensation	Feeling-Sensation
Sensation-Thinking	Sensation-Thinking
Thinking-Sensation	Thinking-Sensation

When the scores are plotted on the graph it becomes immediately apparent whether the psychic energy of the person tested flows inward (Introversion) or outward (Extraversion). It can also be determined which of the four functions is the primary one and which is the auxiliary. For example, an individual may score as follows: I 14 E 20; U 19 S 7; T 10 F 12. He would then be categorized as an Extraverted-Intuitive-Feeling type. It is obvious from the recorded scores that his primary function is Intuition and his auxiliary function is Feeling, since his score on Intuition projects much farther into consciousness than does his score on Feeling.

PRINCIPLES OF INTERPRETATION AND DESCRIPTION OF FUNCTION

Since Dr. Jung's book on psychological types first appeared, there have been many misinterpretations, assigned meanings, and insertion of divergent opinions in discussions of his type theories. In this manual we shall attempt to discuss the six traits with two important prerequisites in mind. First, consideration is given to ensuring an exposition of the six variables as close to Jung's original delineation and description of them as possible. In this we are aided by the long association with Jung, both as pupils and Jungian analysts of two of the survey's authors (Joseph B. Wheelwright and Jane H. Wheelwright) and by the fact that the other author is also a Jungian analyst (Horace Gray). Secondly, the type theory was derived from normal rather than abnormal people, and this questionnaire is designed not to unearth neuroses but to help people understand their relation to themselves and others. Presence of a neurosis tends to obscure accurate responses.

The two basic attitudes toward life are Extraversion and Introversion. The extravert's libido (or psychic energy or interests) flows outward to the object; objective facts or external happenings are the most important factors of life for him. People, things, and events are endlessly interesting to him and he adapts himself easily and well to his environment. His interest is held and his mind stimulated by the object; he reacts to it on a specific basis and does not tend to either generalize or introspect from it. He talks fluently, makes friends readily, and is, in general, a useful and appreciated member of society.

The libido of the introvert is directed predominantly inward, not outward. For the introvert, the significance of the object lies not in itself, but in how it relates to his own psychology. It is not the situation objectively considered, but the situation as he reacts to it that is the dominating factor. The introvert is never completely at home in the external world of men and things, but prefers his own inner life where he is quite at ease. He cannot only endure solitude to a degree that would break the extravert: he must have a considerable amount of it for his mental health. Outer activities may be difficult for him, but he has a rich inner world where he feels at home. The normal introvert also cultivates friends, but tends to limit them in number. It might be said that he forms vertical (depth) relationships as opposed to the horizontal (breadth) relationships of the extravert.

The two modes of perception are Sensation and Intuition. These two alternatives are nonrational functions, not that they are contrary to reason, but that they are outside the province of reason and therefore not established by it.

The term "Sensation" as used here refers to sense perception, that is through the five senses. The sensation type perceives mostly through his senses: outer and inner spontaneously sensed convictions constitute reality for him. He perceives these realities as they exist now, in the present.

The intuitive's psychological function transmits perceptions via the unconscious of the other person. Intuition is an immediate awareness of the whole configuration without a real comprehension of the details of the contents. It concerns itself with inner or outer phenomena. The focus is on possibilities.

Whereas the sensation type is interested in things as they are now, the intuitive sees things as they may be. The solid inner or outer facts of the sensation type tend to be uninteresting to the intuitive, and the possibilities that are so full of life to him have little meaning for the sensation type. The intuitive tends to live in the future or the past, the sensation type in the present. The sensation type depends on concrete data for reaction, the intuitive finds himself hampered by such inflexible matters. The sensation type can't see the woods for the trees; the intuitive can't see the trees for the woods.

Thinking and Feeling are the two functions that are used in an assessing or judging capacity. They are termed rational functions.

Jung considered the thinking individual as one whose every important action proceeds from intellectually considered motives. He meets a situation with logical thought, shaping his actions by its conclusions. Thinking often takes into account the known rules of human experience. Thinking must always be concerned with content, whether inner or outer. It classifies and names: it is impersonal.

Feeling involves an appreciation or depreciation of inner or outer realities. Feeling imparts to the content a definite value in the sense of acceptance or rejection. The feeling function judges by an evaluation of the time, the place, and the person. The feeling function is personal; it represents the individual's acceptance or rejection of something based on his own values but it is also related to its intrinsic worth. The feeling function is chiefly concerned with values and morality—although not necessarily related to conventional attitudes.

The function of the questionnaire therefore is to find which combination is dominant in an individual, and further whether a perceiving or judging function is more readily used. In conclusion. one might consider an individual's reaction to crisis. Does he look around for a way out (Sensation), wait for a hunch (Intuition), think his way out by identifying and analyzing the problem (Thinking), or attempt it through relationship (Feeling)?

HISTORY

Various forms of questionnaires and evaluation sheets making broad distinctions between Introversion and Extraversion have been tried since Jung first published his book on psychological types in 1921. However, none had attempted to separate the four functions and examine their preferential use in the normal personality. This was the aim of the Gray-Wheelwright questionnaire, when it was first formulated in 1944. It seems important to repeat that the authors were Jungian analysts and familiar with type theory both subjectively and objectively.

Three hundred questions were selected and handed out at random, with the invitation to spend twenty minutes in answering. The questions had previously been studied and tentative interpretations of the pair of variables to be measured had been made. The set of replies was compared with clinical estimates of the respondents and progressively pruned, reworded, and restudied. Through a series of sixteen revisions we have arrived at the present questionnaire, and have entitled it the Jungian Type Survey.

USE OF QUESTIONNAIRE

The questionnaire can be of use to any physician or student of personality who wishes to obtain a broad classification of personality characteristics, obtained in a nonjudgmental, nondepreciatory manner.

There are two areas in which a knowledge of psychological types is extremely valuable. In many types of therapy situations, it is helpful to the therapist to estimate the abilities and limitations of patients in terms of their possible behavior and adaptation. The therapeutic process is facilitated if the patient's psychological type is understood by the therapist, and therefore is not allowed to get in the way of therapy. Knowing the psychological type of the person with whom he is talking hopefully makes it more possible for the therapist to speak in a language the patient understands. To talk intuitively to a factual man, or intellectually to a woman who lives through feeling, is a waste of breath.

The second important area is that of marriage relationship. Many vexed marriage situations revolve around type problems that block communications. Our research shows that in a series of more than a thousand subjects a large proportion have married their polar opposites—although for friends they tend to pick similar types. While this "complimentary mating" may produce a total combination of psychological types, it can introduce difficult problems into a marriage. All too often each partner expects his mate's reactions, needs, and desires to be the same as his own. In such a situation, when one assumes that one's partner functions in the same frame of reference that he does, a breakdown in communication usually occurs. This can lead to violent misunderstanding.

A symbiotic relationship can cause a notable blockage of growth. This means that as long as one person can get the other person to perform those functions that he is least capable of performing, he will not develop that side of his personality. In the process of gaining an understanding, not only of one's own psychological type, but also that of one's mate, marriage can become an honest, and realistic relationship. And the growth process is furthered by the necessity to be responsible for one's own inferior functions and their development.

JUNGIAN TYPE SURVEY ANSWER SHEET

Name _____
Occupation _____
Sex _____
Age _____
Marital status _____
Date _____

Scores

I ___ U ___ T ___
E ___ S ___ F ___

Circle each answer a or b

1 ᵃ/b	11 ᵃ/b	21 ᵃ/b	31 ᵃ/b	41 ᵃ/b	51 ᵃ/b	61 ᵃ/b	70 ᵃ/b	78 ᵃ/b
2 ᵃ/b	12 ᵃ/b	22 ᵃ/b	32 ᵃ/b	42 ᵃ/b	52 ᵃ/b	62 ᵃ/b	71 ᵃ/b	79 ᵃ/b
3 ᵃ/b	13 ᵃ/b	23 ᵃ/b	33 ᵃ/b	43 ᵃ/b	53 ᵃ/b	63 ᵃ/b	72 ᵃ/b	
4 ᵃ/b	14 ᵃ/b	24 ᵃ/b	34 ᵃ/b	44 ᵃ/b	54 ᵃ/b	64 ᵃ/b	73 ᵃ/b	
5 ᵃ/b	15 ᵃ/b	25 ᵃ/b	35 ᵃ/b	45 ᵃ/b	55 ᵃ/b	65 ᵃ/b	74 ᵃ/b	80 ᵃ/b
6 ᵃ/b	16 ᵃ/b	26 ᵃ/b	36 ᵃ/b	46 ᵃ/b	56 ᵃ/b	66 ᵃ/b	75 ᵃ/b	81 ᵃ/b
7 ᵃ/b	17 ᵃ/b	27 ᵃ/b	37 ᵃ/b	47 ᵃ/b	57 ᵃ/b	67 ᵃ/b	76 ᵃ/b	
8 ᵃ/b	18 ᵃ/b	28 ᵃ/b	38 ᵃ/b	48 ᵃ/b	58 ᵃ/b	68 ᵃ/b	77 ᵃ/b	
9 ᵃ/b	19 ᵃ/b	29 ᵃ/b	39 ᵃ/b	49 ᵃ/b	59 ᵃ/b	69 ᵃ/b		
10 ᵃ/b	20 ᵃ/b	30 ᵃ/b	40 ᵃ/b	50 ᵃ/b	60 ᵃ/b			

IE

34 32 30 28 26 24 22 20 18 16 14 12 10 8 6 4 2

REFERENCES

Ball, R. J. 1932. Introversion-extroversion in a group of convicts. *J. Abn. & Soc. Psychol.*, 26:422–28.

Campbell, K. J. 1929. The application of extroversion-introversion tests to the insane. *J. Abn. & Soc. Psychol.*, 23:479–81.

Case, V. 1941. *Your Personality, Introvert or Extrovert.* New York: Macmillan.

Cobb, S. 1941. *Foundations of Neuropsychiatry* (2nd ed.). Baltimore: Williams & Wilkins.

Collier, R. M., & Emch, M. 1938. Introversion-extroversion: The concepts and their clinical use. *Am. J. Psychiat.*, 94:1045–75.

Conklin, E. S. 1923. The definition of introversion, extroversion, and allied concepts. *J. Abn. & Soc. Psychol.*, 17:367–82.

———. 1927. The determination of normal extravert-introvert interest differences. *J. Genet. Psychol.*, 34:28–37.

Evans, C., & McConnell, T. R. 1941. A new measure of introversion-extroversion. *J. of Psychol.*, 12:111–24.

Gray, H., & Wheelwright, J. B. 1944. Jung's psychological types and marriage. *Stanford Med. Bull.*, 2:37–39.

———. 1945. Jung's psychological types, including the four functions. *J. Gen. Psych.*, 33:265–84.

———. 1946. Jung's psychological types, their frequency and occurrence. *J. Gen. Psych.*, 34:3–17.

Hinkle, B. M. 1922. A study of psychological types. *Psychoanal. Rev.*, 9:107–97.

Huxley, J. S. 1941. *Man Stands Alone.* New York: Harper.

Jung, C. G. 1923. *Psychological Types.* New York: Harcourt Brace.

Super, D. E. 1942. The Bernreuter personality inventory: A review of research. *Psychol. Bull.*, 39:340–47.

INDEX